MEMOIRS

OF A PHILOSOPHER

Memoirs of a Philosopher

Frederick C. Copleston, S.J.

Sheed & Ward

Sheed & Ward™ is a service of The National Catholic Reporter Publishing Company.

———————

Library of Congress Cataloguing in Publication Data

Copleston, Frederick Charles.
    Memoirs of a philosopher / Frederick C. Copleston.
        p.   cm.
    ISBN 1-55612-570-4
    ISBN 1-55612-621-2 pbk. (alk. paper)
    1. Copleston, Frederick Charles. 2. Historians of philosophy-
-England--Biography. 3. Jesuits--England--Biography.   I. Title.
B51.6.C66A3   1993
192--dc20   93-7810
[B]   CIP

———————

Published by: Sheed & Ward
                115 E. Armour Blvd.
                P.O. Box 419492
                Kansas City, MO 64141-6492

To order, call: (800) 333-7373

Cover art taken from a portrait of Frederick Copleston by William Edward Narraway.

Contents

To the memory of my parents

Acknowledgements

The author wishes to express his warm gratitude and thanks to Father Francis Sweeney, S.J. of Boston College and to Dr. Robert O'Neill, Burns Librarian of the same College, and to John Atteberry, Senior Reference Librarian at Burns, who, in spite of their professional commitments, have made time to interest themselves in the publication of these *Memoirs* and to perform the tiresome and time-consuming work of preparing the manuscript for publication. The author is also privileged to express his gratitude to Mr. Dane Baird, a onetime student of Boston College, whose generosity made possible the publication of this volume.

Foreword

A considerable number of years ago the editorial director of a London publishing firm urged me to compose memoirs. Up to then I had not contemplated undertaking any such activity. A colleague in the University of London had indeed suggested that I should write an account of my life, but I did not pursue the matter, as I thought it highly unlikely that anyone would be interested in reading the account. However, after the publisher had pressed me to compose a book of memoirs I used leisure time in the course of a number of years to write an autobiography. Like John Locke's famous *Essay,* it was written by 'incoherent parcels,' and it would obviously have to be revised or rewritten if there was any serious plan to publish it. Not wishing, however, to waste time on rewriting unless there was reason to suppose that the result would see the light of day, I submitted a large part of what I had written to the successor of the editorial director who had originally suggested that I should undertake the task of writing memoirs. I made it clear, I think, that I was looking for critical evaluation rather than seeking publication of the memoirs as they stood. In other words, did it seem that the typescript could form the basis for a publishable version? If so, I would set my hand to the job. If not, I would avoid wasting further time.

Eventually the editorial director returned the manuscript to me with the comment that the contents were not 'dramatic' enough to ensure a wide sale and that I did not reveal sufficient of myself. Though I was a little annoyed that I had spent valuable time to no good purpose, I had no wish to dispute the editor's verdict. The life of an academic is rarely 'dramatic,' and I have not walked (nor wished to walk) in the corridors of power. Nor had I any desire to perform the kind of striptease act which some modern writers of autobiographies seem to delight in performing. So I decided not to approach any other potential publisher, at any rate for the present.

In advanced years, feeling that I had had quite enough of philosophy and that I no longer had either the capacity or the desire to begin any further serious book on a philosophical topic or on the historical development of philosophical thought, I amused myself by composing a series of bits and pieces, of general reflections on various subjects, including themes related to what is often described as 'spirituality' or 'spiritual life.' My reflections seemed to me banal and hackneyed, but I was glad to express my thoughts on paper, even though I did not attempt to publish any of them, either as articles or in the form of a book.

A Jesuit colleague, however, suggested that I should rewrite my abandoned memoirs, incorporating in the text some of the 'musings' of my later years. For a man who has devoted so much time to writing it is hard to abandon all literary activity. And the proposal attracted me. Even if the result of such activity never saw the light of day, I should at any rate have been occupied in a more or less systematic attempt to get my life into focus and to reflect on basic attitudes. As for the decision about publishing or not publishing any parts or the whole of what I have written, I am quite content to leave this to the relevant authorities of the Society of which I have been a member. It may very well turn out that I am unable to finish the work. But even if I am able to complete it, an old man's reflections are likely to be 'behind the times.' Whether they are void of truth-value is, of course, another question.

Chapter 1

Early Days

IF I TRY TO CONJURE UP PICTURE-MEMORIES OF EARLY childhood, there are some scenes which come to mind, though why these particular scenes and not others, I do not know. For example, I retain an image of snow on the stable roof, glimpsed presumably from my bed on a Christmas morning. Or so memory suggests. Again, I have a clear visual recollection of tortoiseshell butterflies fluttering about on the east window of Trull church in the spring, though this memory must obviously come from a time when I was old enough to be taken to a Sunday morning service. Another image, however, must refer to a pretty early period in my life. It is a picture of myself being with my mother in our brougham, being driven along a central street in Taunton by the coachman whom we employed in those distant days. My mother told me to lie down on the floor of the carriage, so that I should not be seen by the two suffragette ladies who were passing. What action a suffragette might have wanted to take on the sight of a small boy I cannot imagine. I also see myself as a boy of, I suppose, seven being sent by a teacher to the headmistress of a kindergarten, Miss Primrose, for not having properly learned a French ditty (*sur le pont d'Avignon*). Miss Primrose had a visitor with her at the time, and she remarked simply that I had better stay behind at the end of school and try to learn the poem in question.

My father, Frederick Selwyn Copleston, entered the Indian civil service in 1873 and was stationed first as assistant magistrate at Allahabad. In the following year he moved to Burma, where he was eventually appointed Chief Judge of the High Court at Rangoon. His first wife died in 1895, and in 1902 he married my mother, daughter of Colonel Charles Little, a medical officer who was also stationed in Burma. My father planned to return to England after his second marriage; but, according to my mother, the Viceroy, Lord Curzon, asked him to stop on for a couple of years as Governor of Burma. My father refused, and eventually the Viceroy, annoyed at being thwarted, crossed my father's name off the honours list. I do not remember ever having heard my father refer to this episode. He was a reserved man and unlikely to allude to such matters. My information comes simply from my mother.

My father's elder brother, Reginald Stephen, was Anglican Bishop of Calcutta and Metropolitan of India, while another brother, Ernest Arthur, was Anglican Bishop of Colombo. Reginald wrote a book on Buddhism in Ceylon, which, I am told, is still respected. I remember that when I was teaching at the Gregorian University in Rome, I was invited to the British Embassy reception for Geoffrey Francis Fisher, Archbishop of Canterbury, when he came to visit the Pope. On my being presented to him, Fisher remarked that he had known my uncle Reginald and added that I was a 'renegade.' I thought this a very odd remark to make to a person met for the first time, but I refrained from comment and went off to talk to Fisher's chaplain, who was a cousin of mine by marriage.

On their return to England my parents lived for a while in a largish house near Horsham, but they then bought a house in the parish of Trull near Taunton in Somerset, and it was there that I was born on the 10th of April, 1907. My brother Ernest was born two and a half years later. There were no other children. Life was typical of an upper middle-class family of the time, with the usual domestic staff. When my brother and I were small, there was also a 'nannie.' There was a largish garden with tennis court, croquet lawn, flowerbeds of course, a vegetable garden, raspberry and gooseberry plantations, while peaches, nectarines and greengages grew along walls exposed to the sun. We had a permanent gardener, assisted by a youth. And while I was a small child there was a coachman who looked after the horse and drove the trap and, for visiting other families or the town, the brougham. Nowadays all this apparatus seems very far away, something which has receded into the past.

The Copleston family came originally from Devonshire, and we had some cousins not far off, as the living of Offwell and Widworthy, over the border from Somerset, had been occupied by a member of the family from 1773. I remember being taken as a small boy for a walk in the woods at Offwell and seeing the skins of adders hanging from the branch of a tree. One of the more distinguished members of the family to occupy the post of Rector of Offwell (though only for a short period), was Edward Copleston (1776-1849), who became Provost of Oriel College, Oxford, in 1814 and Dean of Chester in 1826, appointments which he resigned in 1828, when he became Bishop of Llandaff and Dean of St. Paul's, London, posts which he held until his death. This combination of high offices would hardly be looked upon nowadays with favour, but I understand that at the time the bishopric of Llandaff was regarded as a kind of waiting-room on the way up the ladder of preferment, and that financial provision was so meagre that unless the occupant of the see was wealthy, he had to have an additional post, which could then be relinquished if he lived to be appointed to a bishopric such as Durham or Winchester.

Though in my branch of the family the spelling of the family name became standardized as 'Copleston,' it has been spelt in various ways at different times. Indeed, I have seen a copy of a will of 1637 in which the name was spelt in several different ways in the same document. It by no means follows, therefore, that if the name is spelled 'Copplestone' (as with the Devonshire village once connected with the family) or 'Coplestone,' the bearer of the name is not a relative of some sort. For my own part, I do not know much about the family history, except that it seems to go back before the Conquest; but a cousin, Mrs. Muriel Reson, who knows a great deal about the subject, has unearthed a large number of family connections in various parts of England and in the United States and Canada. While the family has never been particularly distinguished or famous, it is certainly old.

A feature of my boyhood which I greatly enjoyed were the family picnics. Sometimes we went to the Quantocks, but usually we went somewhere on the Blackdown Hills, which offered at that time (and perhaps, to some extent, even now), completely unspoiled country and magnificent views. Round about the time of the first world war or directly after it my father had a car made to his specifications. It was a remarkable vehicle. A lot of brass and wood work, two cushioned seats in front, like armchairs, for my parents, and a dickey behind. There was also a small folding seat in front. When the hood was up because of rain, the person in the dickey was exposed to the weather. But I quite enjoyed being in the dickey, and if the weather was bad I slipped down into the hold beneath and peered out at the passing countryside. I do not say 'quickly passing,' as my father maintained that fifteen miles an hour was the proper cruising speed, and it was only on rare occasions that we attained the thrilling speed of twenty or even twenty-one miles an hour. The car was very heavy and when we came to a steep hill, all except my father got out. My brother and I gave a shove to the monster, and my mother, brother and I walked up the hill to the spot where we found my father letting the steam out of the radiator. Meeting any other vehicle or a herd of cows or flock of sheep in a narrow Devon or Somerset lane was quite an experience.

In general, I retain happy memories of my childhood. Tea in the garden on hot afternoons, with Red Admirals, Peacocks, Tortoiseshell and other butterflies feeding on the flowers, picnics on the Blackdown Hills, cycling, when old enough, through the charming countryside and old world villages, visits in the summer to seaside resorts such as Seaton, Budleigh Salterton and other places which, in those far off days, were not crowded with coaches and trippers. At the same time I was a very shy boy. This affected my prowess at tennis. I was never good at the game, but in the family circle I could play reasonably well, whereas at a tennis party my play tended to go to pieces. Shyness also inhibited me at dances, when I was old enough to go to them, and I generally found myself taking into supper some unattractive girl whose company was not sought by anyone else. I was happy in the family circle and did not care for parties. I dare say that my parents could have done more to counteract this shyness on my part; but my father did not believe in coercion (or at any rate he did not practice it), and I went to parties and dances only when it could not be avoided without rudeness.

On Sundays we all went to the local parish church at Trull, with its magnificent rood-screen and pulpit. My father was a 'twicer.' That is to say, he attended both Mattins and Evensong. He generally went to the Communion service as well, whether it was at eight in the morning or, on certain Sundays, after Mattins. The rest of the family, however, tended to take the view that attendance at Evensong was not a necessity. For a good many years my father acted as People's Warden, and he proved a thorn in the side to one incumbent, whose ideas he seemed to like opposing pretty well on principle.

My father conducted family prayers before breakfast. This was quite an affair. The gong rang, and the indoors staff made its appearance, taking their places on one side of the dining-room, the cook at one end of the row and the kitchenmaid at the other. My father read a passage from the Bible out loud, and then we all knelt while some prayers were said. If my father happened to be away, my mother or I, when I was old enough, functioned in his place. Whether the servants liked this performance or not, I do not know. Nor, of course, were they asked. However, the ceremony was not a long one. I forget when the practice was dropped; perhaps when my father was showing evident signs of old age. It certainly lasted as long as I was living at home. And I shall have occasion to refer again later on to this family custom. My father doubtless inherited it from his father, who had been a clergyman, and in the absence of any memory to the contrary I assume that my episcopal uncles kept up the same sort of practice.

After his retirement from the ICS my father took part in a considerable number of voluntary and unpaid activities. He was a justice of the peace and was regular in attendance at the appropriate sessions of magistrates; he functioned as a member of the local hospital committee; he actively supported the golf club; and he interested himself in diocesan affairs. If I remember correctly, he was for a time a member of the Anglican House of Laity. Though, however, he was addicted to regular church-going and to maintaining the tradition of family prayers, I recollect his dropping an occasional remark which suggested that he was not so orthodox or traditional in belief as one might suppose. And in his last years he showed, as far as I am aware, no very evident signs of interest in religion. I gathered from my mother that he had been a bit wild in his younger days, and I think it quite likely that his religiousness diminished as he grew older. If so, I feel that I take after him, as I admit with shame that religious services tend to bore me nowadays, and I have some sympathy with the attitude of Immanuel Kant in this matter, even though I do not agree with the German philosopher's one-sidedly moralistic interpretation of religion.

From time to time, of course, relatives came to visit us. My Uncle Reginald, the former Bishop of Calcutta, was always treated with deference and respect. He was a conscientious man, and one would hear him reading the Prayer Book offices daily in his room. His wife, my Aunt Edith, was a daughter of Archbishop Trench of Dublin and was as absent-minded as her father seems to have been. It is said, for example, that when she and my uncle were dining out at someone's else's house in Calcutta, she forgot where she was and said to my uncle across the table, 'we must really change the cook, my dear; this soup is quite tasteless.' On another evening she went out to dinner quite forgetting that she had invited a number of guests to her table. When my uncle returned and lived at Putney, he tried to keep Aunt Edith in order. He used, I believe, to present his annual pension to the diocese of Calcutta, and, in order to practise economy, he forbade his wife ever to supply Devonshire cream in the house. As the good lady was fond of cream, she liked visiting us at Taunton, where she got plenty.

My uncle Ernest, who succeeded Reginald in the see of Colombo (where he suffered a serious fall down part of his cathedral tower) was another respected visitor. But my uncle Edward, who was not a bishop but only a simple parish clergyman, was not treated with much deference. Besides, he used to exasperate my father by his pedantry. Thus he seemed to expect my father to know the exact number of paces required to get from our house to Trull church. How could my father have made this journey so frequently without having ever counted the number of paces needed to traverse the distance? My father did not appreciate such questions. For his part, Uncle Edward became a bit irritated by his wife's (Aunt Alice's) habit of addressing him sweetly as 'my little man' and generally mothering him.

Reginald, Ernest and Edward were all my father's brothers. On my mother's side her parents were also regular visitors. My grandmother used to irritate my father, but my brother and I greatly enjoyed her company. She spoiled us, of course, but she could be very amusing, though not always intentionally. Thus she had the habit, when someone was introduced to her, of extending a couple of fingers and giving a hearty peal of laughter, which tended to embarrass the other person and in any case caused my brother and myself ill-suppressed fits of giggling. In public places such as theatres and restaurants she was inclined to comment, in what she fondly imagined to be a whisper, on anything which attracted her attention, the presence, for instance, of a coloured person.

This habit caused me considerable embarrassment. But Grannie was the soul of generosity, and we boys were delighted when she came to stay and gladly visited her and grandfather.

My mother had a brother, my Uncle Gerald, who was a cheery individual and pleased us boys by buying us sweets. My father was a non-smoker and thought that smoking, if it took place at all, should do so in a special room. As open smoking in a bedroom was regarded as dangerous or decadent or both, Uncle Gerald was reduced to smoking up his bedroom chimney. I never knew him well, as he died when I was still young.

I do not remember when I learned to read, but it must have been at home. Anyway, when I was seven, I was sent on weekdays to a kindergarten maintained by a Miss Primrose, to whom I have already referred. I do recollect having persuaded my mother to invite one or two of the young mistresses to tea. I am afraid that they were treated rather patronizingly, though perfectly politely.

At the age of nine I was sent to a boarding-school, a preparatory school named Naish House, at Burnham-on-Sea, Somerset. It is a rather curious habit of the English upper middle class to send their children away from home at a tender age. The children of the so-called working class are spared this ordeal. One got used to it, of course; but leaving the family nest was always somewhat of a wrench for me. I dare say that the ensuing sink-or-swim situation teaches one to stand on one's own feet, as has been claimed, and also to conceal one's emotive reactions. Whether the latter is altogether beneficial is another question. In any case I have sometimes wondered whether the experience of being extruded, so to speak, even if only temporarily, from the family nest, may not have had an effect on my attitude to the family. I have from time to time idly wondered whether I would have become Catholic, against the wishes of my parents, had I remained longer in the family circle without long periods of absence. Obviously, I do not and cannot know the answer. For all I know, any speculation in which I indulge may be devoid of any firm basis.

As preparatory schools go, Naish House was doubtless a competent institution. That is to say, it prepared pupils adequately for entrance to Public Schools. I remember learning some Latin and mathematics and also French, for reading purposes at any rate. And the English master was certainly an able teacher. To be sure, his claims to have played cricket for Kent or to have tutored the Archbishop of Canterbury or some such august personage were doubtless bogus. Moreover, one day the police came to arrest him on a charge of stealing from the till in a local public house. If I remember right, a fight ensued in the headmaster's study. The good man, who was no fool, defended himself in court and was acquitted (I dare say there was only the barmaid's testimony against him), though in later years one of the relevant magistrates made it clear to me that the Bench were really convinced of the defendant's guilt, even if the evidence was insufficient. Though, however, the man had his shortcomings, he was undoubtedly good at his job, and useful in a variety of ways. Thus he was particularly adept at putting on Gilbert and Sullivan operettas, and he painted the scenery himself. But after the public house episode his career as a schoomaster came to an end. Years later I was waiting for a train on Reading railway station when I was recognized by an army officer who had been a fellow pupil of mine at Burnham-on-Sea. He told me that he had just crossed from one station to another in London, and that when paying off his taxi-driver, he had found him to be the master in question, who had obviously adopted another occupation.

In my last year or so at Naish House my class included A.S.C. Ross. He was at the top of the form, of course, and we called him 'the professor.' This was indeed what he eventually became, distinguishing himself by his reflections on 'U' and 'non-U' in the use of the English language.

At Naish House I took riding lessons as an extra. My favourite mount was a black pony called Joey. It had thrown me at first, but I got to like riding it, and I greatly enjoyed cantering along the sands. Since those days, however, I have not ridden, and I do not know whether the art remains with one or whether one would have to start all over again. Not that I have any intention of experimenting. It was also at Naish House that I learned to swim, in the school swimming-bath, that is to say, not in the Bristol Channel, the water of which recedes for a long distance at low tide, leaving a dreary expanse of mudflats beyond the sand. As for team-games, we played rugger and cricket, but I never shone. It is true that on one occasion I caught a good catch at mid-on, but this was an act of intuitive self-protection and certainly not due to skill. Sammy Woods, the famous Somerset cricketer, occasionally did a little coaching at the school; but I did not merit his services, being the sort of boy who is placed at long stop and keeps out of the way as much as he can.

Of the first world war, which covered my time at Naish House, I remember relatively little. My father was well over military age, but he joined the territorials and acted as a corporal. The family used to see him marching sometimes on a Sunday afternoon, and occasionally he went to a camp. He was also a member of a magistrates' tribunal which functioned when conscription was introduced. There was a confectioner in the town who always showed great signs of deference to my father if he happened to meet him in the street. The family used to maintain that this was because my father, anxious that there should be at any rate one remaining shop in the town where he could purchase sweets, had exempted the gentleman from military service. Apart from such incidents, I have little but vague memories of such things as the spy mania and of the report that hordes of Russians were passing through Taunton station on their way to the western front. Why our gallant Russian allies should be passing through Taunton in particular was left unexplained.

To this day, however, a picture occasionally recurs to my mind of the then headmaster of Naish House entering the classroom on the morning of November 11, 1918, and telling us that an armistice had been signed, and that the rest of the day was free. We were naturally all glad to have a bit of a holiday, and a number of the boys, I remember, expressed pleasurable anticipation of the return of delicacies such as meringues and eclairs with real cream. Though there may well have been, and probably were some boys in the school who belonged to families which had lost a member or members to the 'pale battalions' of what the poet C.H. Sorley called the 'millions of the mouthless dead,' I have no distinct recollection of them. And one would hardly expect a group of small boys to be preoccupied with this aspect of the war on Armistice Day, unless some personal loss was heavy on their minds. My father, as one might expect, was deeply patriotic and a convinced upholder of the Empire, and I, of course, shared his attitude. I am sure that all of us pupils at Naish House were proud and delighted that the Allies had brought Germany to acknowledge defeat. The Boche had been given what was coming to him, and that was a matter for rejoicing and also, or so our elders and betters seemed to believe, for thanksgiving to God, who had helped the righteous cause to triumph. It is only in later years that I have come to be revolted by and look with horror on the senseless and monstrous slaughter of the First World War. What madness! There was, indeed, a good deal of initial enthusiasm, coupled with an expectation of speedy victory. And to see the war as a monument to human folly is not, I hope, to deny or belittle the heroism and self-sacrifice shown by combatants on both sides. But however much I may disagree with some aspects of Bertrand Russell's philosophizing, I find myself in wholehearted sympathy with his basic attitude to the 1914-1918 war. I do not think that its patent irrationality and the horrible slaughter which it involved can be successfully excused by any reference to the dialectic of history. To say this, however, is obviously to go beyond the probable reactions of a small boy's mind, especially if he belongs to the winning side.

As for religion, in these early years I simply accepted the Anglican Christian tradition in which I was brought up. I do not recollect having given much, if any, thought to the matter. I was not in any way precociously 'religious,' but neither was I anti-religious. I was an Englishman and a Christian; religion of a gentlemanly type was simply part of life. It is true that for some reason or other I was put in the school choir at Naish House. I find it difficult to understand why. For I am an extremely bad singer, so bad that the word 'singer' is hardly applicable at all. I can only suppose that I did little more than move my lips in unison with my companions, hoping for the best. Anyway, my inclusion in the choir did not signify any particular religiosity on my part, none that I can remember at any rate.

Chapter 2

Public School

IN 1920, WHEN I WAS THIRTEEN, I ENTERED MARLBOROUGH College in Wiltshire. My father had been there before me. In his days it must have been an extremely tough school. It was tough enough in my time, as far as material amenities were concerned. But from the academic point of view it was an excellent school. Cyril Norwood was headmaster (technically, Master of Marlborough) at the time, and he developed a system of increasing specialization which certainly produced remarkable results in the obtaining of scholarships at Oxbridge. To be sure, if one looks at the matter from the point of view of general education for life, it is clearly questionable whether in their last years at school boys should be concentrating pretty well exclusively on a single subject, such as classics or mathematics or physical science. To know a lot of Greek and Latin while remaining practically completely ignorant of science and unable to speak any language but one's own is not an ideal situation. And analogous remarks can be made in regard to intensified specialization in mathematics or science. However, the specialization policy, which was a conspicuous feature of Norwood's reign, undoubtedly paid dividends when it was a question of university scholarships.

Did I enjoy my time at Marlborough, 1920-25? I do not find it an altogether easy question to answer. I did not enjoy life in the way in which the heroes of cricket and football presumably enjoyed it. But I was certainly not miserable. John Betjeman, a fellow Marlburian, has spoken of boredom as one of his chief impressions. Well, I am pretty sure that I looked forward to the end of my schooldays, and I suppose that this indicates a certain measure of boredom or impatience. But I took things more or less as they came. And while I would certainly not feel inclined to describe my five years at Marlborough as the happiest years of my life, it would be absurd to speak of the period as equivalent to residence in Dachau or a Siberian labour camp. When I first went to the school and was in a junior house, I acquired some reputation as a wag, strange as this may seem to those who have known me in later life. But it was not long before I became more and more interested in religion and religious themes. This rather set apart or tended to confine me to a narrow circle, and I was doubtless regarded as somewhat eccentric, especially when I went in for High Church antics in the chapel. But I do not recollect having incurred any hostility on this account. By and large the boys were very tolerant.

In my time at school great emphasis was laid on games considered likely to foster and manifest team-spirit. As far as I can remember, tennis and golf were frowned on, though squash was regarded as perfectly reputable. Apart from organized games we did a lot of running over the downs or in Savernake Forest. There were official runs, on which we had to reach a certain place by a certain time. I think that the last boy back at College from an official run may have been subject to some punishment, but I am not sure of this. In any case most of us were eager to get back before the supply of hot water gave out. In my senior house at least we did not enjoy the luxury of baths. We stood naked at a row of basins in a room with a concrete floor and bathed in this way. As the hot water tended to give out after a time, we naturally did not need dire threats to get back reasonably quickly from official runs in the rain. These official runs were rather a trial, but they were doubtless good for us. And when I was sufficiently advanced in seniority to be pretty well free, by convention if not by law, from organized games, I used to run a good deal for exercise. I remember running five times in one week to Martinsell. It was a considerable distance, but I enjoyed the magnificent view from the hill over the Pewsey valley. The Marlborough downs may have been rather barren in comparison with the South downs in Sussex, but I have pleasant memories of their open spaces and vistas.

A number of my school fellows were to become eminent or well known in later years. John Betjeman, the future Poet Laureate, was one of them. He was regarded as somewhat eccentric, but he had a fine sense of humour. If I remember correctly, he and his group started to issue a magazine with the motto 'upon Philistia will I triumph.' It did not last long, however. It was, I suppose, too outspoken and provocative for some minds, too at variance with what was taken to be the spirit of the school and the appropriate set of attitudes for young English gentlemen. In his deservedly popular poem 'The Sound of Bells' Betjeman admirably depicted or suggested certain aspects of Marlborough life. At school I knew and liked Betjeman, but I did not belong to his group of aesthetes or intellectuals, and so I saw little of him. At a much later period, when I was lecturing at the old Heythrop College in the Cotswolds and John and his wife Penelope had a house near Wantage, I used occasionally to go over for a Sunday lunch; and it was at Penelope's instigation that I was invited to be among the robed clergy at the memorial service for John in Westminster Abbey, a privilege which I greatly valued.

Louis MacNeice, the poet, was also a schoolfellow. Unless my memory is at fault, we were once in the same form, but I knew him only in the way in which one inevitably becomes acquainted with contemporaries whose school studies overlap with one's own. I never knew MacNeice well; our interests were too different for friendship (which does not imply that we were enemies, of course).

Notable among future celebrities was Anthony Blunt. For a boy still at school he had a remarkable knowledge of Renaissance art, and hindsight enables one easily to discern the future art historian. Needless to say, the future Soviet agent was not discernible, not by me at any rate. It was at Cambridge, not Marlborough, that Blunt fell victim to Communist blandishments. But he was senior to me at school, and I really knew him only by sight and reputation. Whereas Betjeman was extremely approachable and forthcoming, Blunt gave the impression of looking down his nose at the vulgar herd, which would certainly include religious fanatics such as myself. In the seventies I met a Swiss lady who had studied art under Blunt at the Cortauld Institute, and she paid tribute to him as a superb teacher. If only he had kept exclusively to his work as an art historian.

Among personal friends were John Parker and Christopher Hussey. John Parker was to become active in the Fabian Society and was for many years Labour Member of Parliment for Dagenham, ending his political career as 'Father of the House.' On retirement he should have been given a seat in the Lords, where he would doubtless have continued to do a lot of useful work. At school he studied history, and I remember him delivering long discourses on some phase of history, say early Byzantine history, discourses which, though admirably learned, could be a trifle irritating on a country walk. In my last year at Marlborough I shared a study with John and with another boy who became a clergyman and whose name I have unfortunately forgotten. After our Marlborough schooldays John and I were both undergraduates of St. John's College, Oxford, and I remember that in the first two years, when we were both living in College, we sometimes (often?—I don't recollect) breakfasted together on Sundays. A certain 'Don,' however, advised John not to see much of me, as frequent consorting with an ardent convert to Catholicism would not do him any good. In any case John became increasingly involved in Labour politics in university life, and he naturally gravitated to the company of undergraduates such as Michael Stewart, the future Labour Foreign Secretary.

Christopher Hussey was the son of an Anglican Canon at Northampton and elder brother of the Hussey who became Dean of Chichester and a noted patron of modern artists. Thus it was for the younger Hussey's church at Northampton that Henry Moore made a magnificent Madonna and Child, which occupied a prominent place in the exhibition of the sculptor's works at the Royal Academy of Arts in 1988. Christopher Hussey, John Parker and I may possibly have been, in some respects, an ill-assorted trio, but at one time at any rate we took frequent walks together at Marlborough. We discovered a place called 'The Who would have Thought It?' in a village in the downs; and when we had sufficient funds, we had an ample tea (at, I think, one and sixpence a head) in the parlour of the proprietress and solved the problems of the world. Christopher became an extremely High Church Anglican clergyman. In later years I visited him once in his parish on the Isle of Dogs, where the then Bishop of London seems to have placed him with the idea that Christopher could not do much harm down there. When I visited him, he showed me his church and remarked that they had recently sung a Te Deum there. On my asking why, he replied that the Cardinal Archbishop of Westminster had ordered the singing of a Te Deum in his diocese in thanksgiving for some event which I do not remember. I gathered that it was the Archbishop of Westminster rather than his own Bishop of London that Christopher prayed for at the appropriate place in the Canon of the Liturgy. His younger brother, the Dean of Chichester, was a man of wider interests.

In my senior house at Marlborough there were, if I remember correctly, three brothers called Mason, the youngest being James, the future cinema star. I remember that the eldest brother, a very nice boy, was the benevolent captain of my dormitory. James was considerably junior to me, and I hardly knew him. In fact I would hesitate to mention him as a schoolfellow if I did not remember G.C. Turner, my former housemaster, referring to James Mason when I visited him in his retirement (after being Headmaster of Charterhouse) at Chichester.

I suppose that in any account of one's time at a Public School, one may be expected to allude to three particular subjects, food, corporal punishment and sex. In my opinion quite enough has been written on these themes without my adding to the relevant literature, but I do not want to give the impression of studiously avoiding any mention at all of the topics in question. So I risk a few banal remarks.

As for food, we were certainly not starved, but the food was extremely stodgy, not exactly what one would expect in a leading French restaurant. But nobody in his senses would expect it to be, and, within limits, we probably liked having something heavy, believing that there was 'body' in it and that it keep us in good condition for our athletic exertions. However, there were some limits. Boys in the in-College houses took their meals in a common Hall, and for tea we were given thick ship's biscuits. In order to be able to get our teeth into them we soaked them in the tea. After a while more palatable biscuits made their appearance. But the boys ate these, of course. And so we returned to our previous fare. Popular comment can be imagined. In point of fact, however, boys tended not to go to Hall for their tea, unless they happened to have run out of pocket-money. We went to one of the cafes on the edge of the small town and consumed cream cakes and buns, ices in the summer. When we became senior enough to share a study, we generally had tea in our studies, and often Sunday breakfast as well, cooking bacon or sausages over gas-rings. I always enjoyed these meals in studies, especially in summer. During winter it was rather cold, as the heating-system left a lot to be desired, though I dare say that having to rough it a bit did us good.

In his reminiscences of Marlborough life Sir John Betjeman refers not only to boredom but also to fear of beatings. In regard to the second subject my own memories of the school suggest that in most Houses it was quite possible to get through one's school career without being beaten by one's housemaster. For, generally speaking, one knew what sort of action or conduct would incur a beating. One might, indeed, have bad luck, but it would be a gross exaggeration to accuse all Marlborough housemasters of being ardent sadists. In my own House the boys used to say of G.C. Turner that if he proposed to beat a boy in the morning, he spent the night wrestling in prayer with his Maker. While I do not suppose that this story was literally true, it expressed the boys' intuitive recognition that when Turner had recourse to corporal punishment, he did so because the school conventions demanded it, not because the activity gave him any peculiar pleasure. Again, as Louis MacNeice relates in his book of memoirs (*The Strings are False,* p. 90), there was one housemaster who was popularly said to be too lazy to beat offenders. He used to give them a choice between being beaten and helping him with some chore or other, grinding coffee, for example, or assisting him in his garden. There were, to be sure, some masters of another kind. The most notable example was a housemaster who clearly enjoyed beating boys and who on one occasion at least beat the whole of his House Fifteen for losing a match. By and large, however, it was not really the masters who represented the constant threat to which Betjeman referred. There was considerably more beating of boys by boys than boys by masters. It was not primarily a case of the prefects, who, as 'intellectuals,' tended to think of themselves as a cut above sadistic practices. It was more a question of 'captains' of one sort or another. For example, in my House, groups of younger boys had the job, in rotation, of cleaning the tables on which older boys who did not occupy studies were accustomed to eat various messes in the evenings. The senior boys were always able to find some traces of, say, marmalade, if they wanted to; and as it was hardly possible to determine who was the particular offender out of the group of fags* (at Marlborough there was only corporate, not personal, fagging), the custom was that the fags should suffer in turn, automatically so to speak. Thus however hard a fag might try to do his allotted job, sooner or later his turn for a (not very terrible) chastisement would arrive. Most of us, I am sure, looked on such events as part of life, as something which one put up with in one's junior years and which passed away with advancing seniority. Nobody, as far as I can remember, made a great song and dance about the matter.

These remarks are not intended to imply any enthusiasm on my part for the practice of corporal punishment in schools. As for the beating of boys by boys, this has doubtless relieved masters of most of the responsibility for maintaining discipline and has prevented any efforts at concerted and general rebellion, but even if the practice has proved expedient from the point of view of the school authorities, it is, in my opinion, outdated and quite unsuited to modern society. Boys from public schools are not nowadays sent out to rule despotically over subject peoples, and freedom to beat their fellow pupils seems to me an absurd training for adult life. When I revisited Marlborough from the old Heythrop College to preach in the College chapel, I was pleased to learn from the then headmaster, Mr. Dancy, that he had abolished the practice in question. And when I was entertained to coffee by a house prefect and some senior boys, I was interested to hear them mention the change and express entire agreement with it.

As for the beating of boys by housemasters, a case can doubtless be made out for it, provided that the punishment is inflicted for infringing a known and clearly defined rule and not used as a substitute for good teaching or tuition (or, I would add, for 'moral' offences). After all, if a boy who has been discovered breaking a known and

---

* fag: an English public-school boy who acts as servant to an older schoolmate.

sufficiently clearly defined rule suffers the punishment which he knowingly risked, one might reasonably comment that he has only himself to blame. At the same time, quite apart from the psychological consideration which psychologists are inclined to emphasize and probably sometimes to exaggerate, many modern countries, including the Soviet Union, get along without the practice of corporal punishment in schools; and if the United Kingdom has to be an exception, something is badly wrong with our home training or with the educational system or with both. The argument that corporal punishment toughens the young and turns them into men does not seem very convincing to me. I know of no evidence, that the Russians, for example, are more effeminate than the English. So I find myself in sympathy with the progressive abolition of corporal punishment in the public schools, though I see that a case may be made out in favour of a limited and rational use of it. In other words, while avoiding a dogmatic attitude on the matter, I believe that both in the public schools and elsewhere we should try to get along without corporal punishment. The public schools in which the practice has been allowed to die out or which have abolished it, do not seem to have suffered on this account.

Finally, sex. If anyone were to tell me that the Marlborough College of my time was a hotbed of vice, I would take it that he was one of those people who have an *a priori* idea of how things *must* be and then conclude that this is how things *were* or *are*, as the case may be. To be sure, there were frequent cases of an older boy feeling a romantic attachment to some attractive younger boy. What else would one expect if boys between the ages of thirteen and eighteen or nineteen are segregated for most of the year, especially in the absence of any girls? But, as Betjeman aptly remarked, if such attachments lasted as long as they often did, it was because they rarely led to any results or satisfaction on the physical level. I remember experiencing a long-lived attraction for a younger boy in the same House. But as I was pretty well too shy to address him and he had no interest in me, it was a very one-sided relationship, admitted to and discussed with friends of one's own age but never mentioned to the object of one's affections. The boy in question later became a bishop. There were doubtless some cases of fumbling sexual experimentation, but it seems true to say that for the most part such incidents took place between boys of much the same age and rarely accompanied the romantic attachments referred to above. In general, the stress laid on games and the publicity of life at Marlborough hardly encouraged the development of widespread 'vice.'

Some people seem to think that public school life creates or has created homosexuals out of nothing. While, however, it may well be the case that already existing predispositions can be strengthened and confirmed by the life, the question whether the incidence of homosexuality is greater among those who have been educated at sexually segregated boarding-schools than among those who have been to day schools or to sexually mixed schools is a matter for empirically based inquiry, not for *a priori* dogmatism. If, however, we take it that there are varying degrees, so to speak, of potential bisexuality in the human person and that development in the heterosexual direction is to be encouraged rather than discouraged, it seems to me to follow that a policy of co-education is to be preferred to one of sexual segregation. School education has often been described as a preparation for life; but it is surely part of the process of living rather than simply a preparation for it. And if this is the case, co-education seems to me clearly preferable to sexual segregation. I was glad to learn from Mr. Dancy that he had succeeded in introducing the experiment of including some girls in the higher classes at Marlborough.

To avoid possible misunderstanding, I should like to add that the foregoing remarks should not be understood as expressing a desire to persecute homosexuals or to put the clock back from a legal point of view. It is a question whether sexually segregated communities are a desirable feature in our system of education or at any rate in one prominent part of it. On balance I support the policy of reform, provided that common sense and the lessons of experience are not abandoned or thrown out of the window. My position doubtless presupposes a belief concerning what is more 'natural' and desirable in human life. One can maintain this belief, I hope, without its being accompanied by a desire to persecute homosexuals. But there is no need to enlarge upon the theme here. I have said enough to make my point.

While I feel no urge to embark upon any protracted discussion of the merits and demerits and future of the Public School system, it would certainly seem to me foolish to destroy this institution when its continued life is clearly desired by a section of the population and as long as no really adequate alternative is yet available. In other words, I have scant sympathy with the desire to abolish the Public Schools simply for the sake of abolishing them or, if preferred, for purely ideological reasons. At the same time critics of the Public School system as being increasingly out of tune with modern British society certainly have a strong case and can present arguments which are by no means simply negligible. Change may indeed be desirable, but change should take the form of development of something better than what actually exists, not of depriving boys and girls of educational opportunities. It may well be the case that we need a less class-conditioned system of education, but progress cannot be achieved by lowering standards and penalizing the more intellectually promising youth of the country. What we need is to spread more widely the educational facilities offered by the better Public Schools, not to bring everyone down to the lowest common level. This is simply a matter of common sense, I would have thought; but some wild persons seem, in effect, to take a different view.

During my years at Marlborough I moved progressively towards the Catholic Church, becoming a Catholic while still at school. As I propose to treat this matter in the next chapter, I will make no further allusion to it here except to say that my religious preoccupations affected my studies adversely, for good or for bad as the case may be. My mind was directed to other fields than the niceties of classical scholarship; and the fact that I was pursuing a line of action which would cause considerable distress to my parents and run contrary to their will and to that of the school authorities was hardly likely to promote peace of mind. As things turned out, however, I left school with a reasonable though certainly limited knowledge of Greek and Latin literature, an ability to read French but not to speak it, acquaintance with English history and literature, and precious little knowledge of either mathematics or science. I enjoyed some English poetry of the romantic variety, and I was strongly attracted by the great Russian novelists, whose works I read in translations. To this day I retain a visual memory of my sitting by a fire in the Bradley Library with other fairly senior boys after a run in the rain, eating hot muffins and reading some Russian novel. As for the classics, we had to read reams at the time, but now I remember only a very few tags or fragments which, for some reason or other, have stuck in my memory. For example, Virgil's *Te, Palinure, petens, tibi tristia somnia portans, insonti.*

While I certainly do not look back on Marlborough as a kind of womb to which I would like to return, no more do I regard it in restrospect with horror or dislike. It seems to me to have been in many ways an excellent school. The emphasis on games did not entail neglect of or contempt for intellectual standards, and there was really plenty of scope for boys to broaden their intellectual outlooks. In more recent days the school has doubtless become a much more humane and civilized place, but, as I have indicated, the tough side of life did not bother me unduly, though I was glad to be in a House (BI) which did not have a sadist as housemaster. Though, however, I feel grateful to Marlborough in a variety of ways, I do not think that I would describe life as I knew it in the first half of the 1920s as an ideal preparation for life in the contemporary world. But something can fail to attain ideal standards without on that account being devoid of real value.

Chapter 3

Becoming a Catholic

I ONCE KNEW A CONVERT TO CATHOLICISM WHO, WHEN asked why he had become a Catholic, was accustomed to answer simply 'the grace of God.' Though, however, this answer may be acceptable from a theological point of view, it is very unlikely that those who ask the question out of curiosity or interest expect or are content to receive a reply which consists in referring to a supernatural phenomenon in which they may not believe. Nor presumably are they asking for the sort of answers which psychoanalysts may propose. It is much more probable that they are asking for the reasons which were present in the convert's mind and of which he or she was aware. They are doubtless inquiring about conscious motivation. To be sure, in trying to recall such reasons one may tend to misrepresent them, to reconstruct them in the light of subsequent experience. But one can at any rate make an effort to recall them; and it is unlikely that one would have entirely forgotten what they were.

One thing at least seems to me certain, namely that as a boy in my last year at Marlborough I very much wanted to be a Catholic, that I felt that I had to become one, that, in theological language, this was God's will for me. Whether it actually was or was not God's will, I at any rate believed that it was. This, I think, is simply a

25

psychological fact. And having come across a priest who was prepared (as most priests in this country would not be) to receive into the Catholic Church a schoolboy not only without the permission of family or school but also against their expressed will, I was conditionally baptized on a July day in 1925 in the chapel of a family who kept a racing stables near Marlborough, two or three months after reaching the age of eighteen.

Marlborough was at that time in the parish of Devizes, and it was the parish priest of Devizes, a Frenchman called Father Louis Valluet, who received me into the Catholic Church. He was a zealous and warm-hearted man. Even the bishop was prepared to recognize his saintliness. But he was no great stickler for regulations. I had talked with him on several occasions. He asked me what the doctrine of the Immaculate Conception was, and, having read a good deal about Catholic doctrine, I knew the answer. So he filled up the requisite form for the bishop, stating that I had received the statutory course of instruction, which was hardly the precise truth. The good man knew, of course, that I had been forbidden to become a Catholic before I had attained the age of twenty-one, but he was eager to get me into the Church, and he told me that though I should inform my parents about my coming reception into the Catholic Church, there was no need to leave them time to do anything effective to prevent it. And in point of fact I presented both my parents and the school authorities with an accomplished fact.

For the benefit of readers who may be inclined to regard the French priest's attitude as typical of the Catholic clergy, I hasten to add that if I had approached any ordinary English priest, I should doubtless have been urged to discuss the matter again with my parents and to arrange for a proper course of instruction extending over the period of time prescribed by the bishop. But it would be unfair to the Frenchman to regard him as an unscrupulous zealot who took full advantage of a schoolboy's enthusiasm and lack of experience and due reflection. In a sense, I suppose, we were a pair. It was not, indeed, simply a case of my deliberately choosing a priest who would give me the advice for which I hoped, much as the young man mentioned by Sartre in his lecture on existentialism and humanism went for counsel to a person who, as he could be pretty sure in advance, would give him the counsel which he wished to receive. For Father Valluet was the local parish priest and one of the very few Catholic priests with whom I was in any way acquainted at the time. It would be quite wrong of me, however, to conceal the fact that I wanted to be received into the Catholic Church while away from home and that I found in Father Valluet the instrument, so to speak, to realize my project. But this is perhaps a rather misleading way of expressing the matter. For it suggests an abundance of cold calculation, whereas in reality there was plenty of ardour, whether misplaced or not.

When I was a small boy living near Taunton, I knew very few Catholics. There were, indeed, social relations between my family and a Catholic family in the neighbourhood. The husband was of Cuban origin. His English wife had become a Catholic, and the children were brought up as Catholics. My brother and I were invited to parties at their house, and they came to us. But though I was aware that they were Catholics and went to the Catholic church in Taunton on Sundays, this knowledge made little impression on me. And I do not recollect any member of the family in question ever raising the question of religion.

We also knew a spinster who was a convert to Catholicism and who, incidentally, was very fond of Bridge parties. When I was walking one day with my mother and saw the good lady approaching us, I asked my mother whether our dog Punch, presumably a good Protestant, was likely to engage in combat with Miss Carew's dog, which I assumed to be a Catholic. But apart from Miss Carew and the family mentioned above, I do not remember coming across any other Catholics while I was a child.

At Marlborough in my time two boys were Catholics. The family of one of them had all become Catholics. He was, I think, the last of them to be received and he was permitted to continue in the school and to go to an early Mass on Sundays at Ogbourne St. Andrew (where the chapel and racing stables were), provided that he put in a physical presence at the obligatory school chapel services. The other boy also used to attend Mass on Sundays, taken by the French wife of one of the masters in her car, but I noticed that he joined actively in the school chapel services, which at that date Catholics were still not supposed to do. Anyway, neither boy was in my House, and I hardly knew either of them.

My point is obviously that it was not the influence of any Catholic friend or acquaintance which originated in me a desire to enter the Catholic Church. When I made the acquaintance of a few priests I had already conceived this desire, at any rate in an initial and preliminary form. Thus during school holidays from Marlborough I used to call on Canon O'Shaughnessy, the parish priest of Taunton at the time. While, however, he certainly encouraged me in my desire to become a Catholic, he was not responsible for its origin. Again, when G.C. Turner, my housemaster at Marlborough, once took a small party of us by car to Oxford, where we went on the river, I managed to find an excuse for absenting myself for a time and paid a call at the then Jesuit church of St. Aloysius, to talk with a priest. Reading the names of the priests on a notice board, I found the name Steuart reassuring and asked for Father Steuart. He turned out to be the writer on mystical subjects, R.H.J. Steuart, and my talk with him helped to confirm me in my desire to become a Catholic, but the thought of becoming a Catholic had obviously preceded and inspired my visit. Then there was, of course, the French priest who eventually received me into the Catholic Church. As we were pretty free to cycle round the countryside on afternoons when there were no classes, I was able to visit him occasionally at Devizes. He struck me as foreign and quaint, and I could not help laughing at some of his ways of expressing himself. But he was clearly good and kind, and I have no doubt that he influenced me. At the same time I do not think that my original interest in Catholicism and the initial desire to become a Catholic were derived from any priest-acquaintance.

What about the liturgical aspects of Catholic worship? Having been accustomed from childhood to the level of Anglican churchmanship represented by surplices, coloured stoles and eastward position, I was indeed, pleasantly excited when I grew old enough to be permitted to make occasional excursions to Anglican churches in Taunton where the eucharistic vestments were regularly used. St. John's church in particular, with its incense, Sung Mass, Solemn Vespers and so on, was more to my taste at the time than what seemed to me the rather tame services at our local church at Trull. At an early age I came to think (rightly) that the Eucharist should be and should be seen to be the central act of Christian worship. This was the period of the so-called Fiery Cross mission, which aimed at converting England to Anglo-Catholicism. Though, however, ceremony and ritual certainly exercised a strong attraction on me at the time, they can hardly constitute an adequate cause of my turn towards the Catholic and Roman Church. For, the use of Latin apart, it was hard to be 'higher' than the Anglican church of St. John at Taunton.

While zealously exploring the local variants of High Church practice, I could not help becoming aware that in the dim background there lurked a Church which was not only the real source of the ceremonies and ritual which at that time appealed to me but also represented authority. I am sure that the authoritarian nature of the Catholic Church, the self-assurance with which Rome spoke, and what I conceived to be the obedient loyalty of its members, were together a powerful source of attraction for me. As I have said, I knew very few Catholics, and my idea of the Catholic Church was based on reading rather than on any personal experience. But this does not affect the fact that I conceived the Church as speaking with the clear voice of authority and as comparing very favourably with the Church of England with its various parties and

with an episcopate which included members whose orthodoxy seemed to be pretty clearly dubious.

There have, of course, been many converts to Catholicism who have been attracted by its authoritarian character. And in this connection it is customary to refer to
the desire for security, and to imply that those who seek
security and find it in the bosom of the Catholic Church
are inadequate human beings, unable to stand on their
own feet and to think for themselves. They therefore
throw themselves into the arms of Holy Mother Church,
who does their thinking for them and simply tells them
what to believe and what to do.

This interpretation of the situation is understandable, and one can hardly exclude the possibility that a desire for security has had something to do with a good
many cases of conversion, including perhaps one's own.
But there are other relevant considerations. It seemed to
me that if Christ was truly the Son of God and if he
founded a Church to teach all nations in his name, it
must be a Church teaching with authority, as her Master
did. Obviously, one might deny that Christ was the Son
of God, and one might reject the claim that he founded a
Church. But if these two claims were accepted, it seemed
to me that in spite of all its faults the Roman Catholic
Church was the only one which could reasonably be
thought to have developed out of what Christ established.
To be sure, my knowledge of the various Christian denominations was extremely limited, and I now see that I
was often unfair not only to religious bodies of which I
knew not only by reading but also to the Church in which
I had been brought up. At the same time it seemed to
me that when it was a question of Christian doctrinal beliefs, it could hardly be a matter simply of private opinion, of what 'one feels' to be or not to be the case. One
could not decide between doctrines relating to the transcendent by empirical testing. Either one should adopt
an agnostic attitude or one should invoke divine revelation mediated by a teaching institution which was
divinely protected from error. This may be an over-sim-
plified view of the matter, but I am simply trying to

illustrate my attitude, as far as I can recapture it, at the time when I was contemplating migrating from the Church of England to the Catholic Church, the Church recognizing the teaching authority of the Pope. For me, Anglicanism formed what might perhaps be described as a point of departure, as something to be left behind and transcended, but not as something to be abandoned in favour of agnosticism.

This idea, namely that any Church founded by the Incarnate Son of God must speak with a clear authoritative voice was by no means the only influential factor in arousing my desire to become a Catholic. When I was still a boy in a junior House at Marlborough and thus about fourteen or possibly fifteen years old, I wrote an essay in which I castigated the Church of England for reducing Christianity to bourgeois mediocrity and for failing to uphold the ideals of the New Testament. I do not remember precisely what I wrote, but I have no doubt that I compared the Church of England with Catholicism to the former's disadvantage. I showed this essay to my housemaster, a Mr. Beecher, who was remarkably patient with me, in spite of my probably intemperate remarks. Anyway, my main point was that though the Church of Rome certainly had its dark aspects (Torquemada, the fires of Smithfield, some of the Popes, and so on), it had at any rate upheld ideals of sanctity and otherworldiness and had not equated true religion with being an English gentleman. At the time I had not heard of Kierkegaard, but my line of thought bore some similarity to his in his attack on the State Church of Denmark.

My attitude was reinforced when I started to read works of Catholic spirituality and mysticism. St. Teresa of Avila and St. John of the Cross opened up for me vistas of a new world, which exercised a powerful attraction on my mind. I was indeed aware, or became aware, that some Anglicans had written profoundly spiritual works. At the same time it seemed to me that mystical religion was a foreign body, so to speak, in the Church of England, and that religiously inclined Anglicans were inclined to turn to Catholic writings, such as the *Imitation of Christ* and books by Père Grou. The atmosphere or tone of Anglicanism, as I had experienced it (and I freely acknowledge the limitations of my experience), seemed to me to be far removed from the sort of ideals which had been exhibited in a concrete manner in the lives of Catholic saints.

Incidentally, the headmaster of Marlborough, Cyril Norwood, unwittingly helped to confirm my impression. For in a sermon in the College Chapel he once stated that honesty compelled him to say that St. John the Evangelist and St. Paul were more akin to Catholic mystics than to Anglican divines. The fact that this statement stuck in my mind shows that it must have attracted my attention and left a strong impression. (Though a 'Modern Churchman,' Norwood greatly respected mystical religion. At the same time he was convinced that it was not suitable for the great bulk of schoolboys. Instead he laid emphasis on the spirit of 'service.')

Looking back on my schooldays, I am probably too much inclined to see myself as following a straight path from the Anglicanism in which I was brought up to Catholicism. By and large, I suppose that it was a question of coming ever closer to Rome. But there were a few excursions or divagations. For example, I was attracted at one time by the ideas of the American writer Ralph Waldo Trine, who offered a popular version of Emerson's religious thought. I probably saw Emerson and Trine as providing what might be described as a short-cut to mystical experience.

However this may be, by the time I was seventeen I had made up my mind to become a Catholic. When I explained this to my father, he was so distressed that I dropped the matter for the time being. I was doubtless told that I should wait until I was twenty-one and then see how I felt about things. But, as I have already said, my desire to take the final step proved too strong for me and, as Father Valluet was prepared to receive me, I became a Catholic not long after turning eighteen.

After the reception ceremony at Ogbourne St. Andrew I cycled back to Marlborough and asked G.C.

Turner, my housemaster, if I might go to Ogbourne St. Andrew the next morning to receive my first communion, as I had just been received into the Catholic Church. He sighed and said 'yes,' adding that he would have to see Cyril Norwood and that I had better wait in his room until he had talked with Norwood. After a while he came back to say that I must leave the school. My father would be arriving the next day. So I should pack and get ready for departure. I was told not to say anything about the matter to the boys in general.

As noted above, at the time I was occupying a study with John Parker and another boy. To celebrate my reception and approaching departure we consumed, I remember, a considerable quantity of raspberries and cream in our study. And the next morning I set about packing my trunk. I was not allowed to sit for that morning's paper in the Higher Certificate examination, and as the paper in question was an essential part of the examination, this meant that I had to forego the Higher Certificate. However, I had already acquired a sufficient number of 'Credits' in the School Certificate to qualify for university entry—supposing that my father were still prepared to send me to Oxford. (Encouraged by Father Valluet, I was ready to abandon the prospect of Oxford and even for being turned out of my home.)

The meeting with my father was, of course, very painful. He was extremely distressed, and he looked on my expulsion as a terrible disgrace to the family. In fact he was so overcome that Norwood, out of consideration for his feelings, said that I could remain at Marlborough until the end of the summer term (not very far away), though he did not consider me as being any more a member of the school. I was not, however, to attend the OTC camp at the end of the term, a deprivation which did not bother me.

Seeing that in the immediate future things were going to be pretty difficult in the family, my housemaster, G.C. Turner, a genuine Christian and good friend, invited me to come for a short motor tour with himself and his brother, who was a Fellow of a Cambridge college, at the end of the term. My brother could go home and prepare the ground, as it were, for my arrival. So off I went with Turner and his brother to such places as Stow-in-the-Wold and Clun in Shropshire. I have never forgotten Turner's thoughtful kindness.

My father neither turned me adrift nor showed any sign at all of contemplating such a move. Indeed, I feel ashamed at ever having thought it possible (if I, in fact, ever seriously thought it possible) that he would act in this way. I doubt whether I ever realized at the time how fond my father was of me and what expectations he entertained in regard to my future. One trouble was that he was not only reserved but also so much older than I was. As for relatives and friends of the family, they naturally thought that I had behaved very callously to my parents, especially to my father, who took my reception into the Catholic Church much more tragically than my mother did. Well, surveying the course of events after so many years, I find myself in agreement with them. Indeed, when in later life I have experienced this or that trial, I have often said to myself something like 'it serves you right for the way in which you treated your parents; you are reaping what you have sown.' I certainly wish now that I had gone about becoming a Catholic in a way less likely to cause pain, distress and bewilderment to others, but if one says 'suppose that I were once more seventeen or eighteen years old, I would have acted rather differently,' is it not a case of sitting in judgement on oneself at a later period of life and taking a dim view of certain past actions in the light of subsequent reflection? In other words, if I were once more seventeen or eighteen years old, placed in precisely the same circumstances, possessing only the same limited experience, with precisely the same character-traits, and subject to the same stimuli, is it not reasonable to suppose that I would act in much the same sort of way? This does not constitute a good reason for refusing to find fault with one's past actions. One can perfectly well regret and disapprove of aspects of one's past conduct. But it does not necessarily follow that if one could go back in time to the relevant situation, one would act differently. If one thinks that one would, is this not because one imports back into one's past attitudes, reactions and judgements which had not been formed or properly developed at the relevant time? The trouble, of course, with this kind of problem is that it can hardly be settled empirically or experimentally. We cannot go back in time and start again.

If anyone feels prompted to ask whether I have ever thought seriously of returning to the Church of England, the answer, as far as I can recollect, is a decided 'no.' I am, of course, well aware that in my youth my attitude to the Anglican Church was one-sided and unfair, exaggeratedly critical. I have great respect for sincere Anglicans, whether clerical or lay, and I have been much impressed by devoted Nonconformist and Presbyterian Christians whom I have come across. But I still believe that the centre of Christian unity is to be found in the Catholic Church, and that though Anglicanism certainly has a contribution to make to Christian life (as, indeed, have other Christian religious bodies too), this contribution should be made through some form of real communion with the Holy See. I should add that in later years it has not been interdenominational problems which have loomed large on my mental horizon but rather what I at any rate would regard as more basic religious themes. But to say more about this subject here would be, I think, anachronistic and inappropriate.

A final note, to bring this chapter to an end. After my reception into the Catholic Church life at home tended to be rather difficult from time to time, especially in view of the ecclesiastical regulations then in force in regard to participation by Catholics in prayers and religious services conducted by members of other communions. When I had become a Catholic and asked the then Bishop of Clifton what I should do in the matter of family prayers, he replied that though I could put in a physical presence, if absence would cause trouble and distress, I must not join in. Being an obedient convert, I complied with this direction. The bishop was only applying regulations, of course, even if in a very literal manner. The regulations, however, now seem to me pretty monstrous. That one should be forbidden even to say the Our Father together with other members of one's family smacks of another and bygone age. Anyway, if present-day attitudes had prevailed at the time, and if I had been able not only to join in family prayers but sometimes at any rate to accompany the rest of the family to Sunday Mattins or Evensong, my parents would have been saved a good deal of pain and family life would have been more harmonious. I do not mean to imply that my parents, or my father in particular, were constantly referring to my having opted out of participation in their religious observances. But the subject naturally tended to come up, especially on Sundays, and my intransigence (highly meritorious, of course, in the eyes of the English Catholic ecclesiastical authorities of the time) certainly pained my father. Some might comment that I have grown lax in my views with the course of years, but when I look back, it seems to me very odd that while I could eat with my family and make expeditions with them, I was supposed not to pray with them or, more accurately, to confine my participation to physical presence. We have made some progress since that time, thank God.

Obviously, there have been other changes in the Church besides the development of a greater openness to manifestations of Christian life outside the Catholic and Roman Church, and if anyone has any interest at all in my religious history, it is natural for him or her to wonder how I, as a convert who was impressed by the authoritarian aspect of the Catholic Church, reacted to such changes. But any remarks on this subject are best reserved for a later stage in this account of my life.

Chapter 4

Four Years at Oxford

IN SPITE OF THE FACT THAT I HAD BECOME A CATHOLIC
against his wishes, my father did not wish to deprive me
of the opportunity of studying at Oxford, though he de-
creased the amount of the allowance which he intended to
give me. So in October 1925 I went up to the university
as a member of St. John's College, where one of my
episcopal uncles had been a Fellow. It seemed to be
taken for granted that I would continue with classical
studies. I do not recollect that any other possibility was
discussed. As I had ended my life at Marlborough in the
classical upper sixth, it seemed only natural, I suppose,
both to myself and to all others concerned that I would
read for Honour Moderations and then 'Greats.' I shall
return presently to the subject of studies.

In those days each undergraduate in College had two
rooms, a bedroom and a living-room. Breakfast, lunch
and tea were brought to one's room by the 'scout' who
looked after the sets of rooms situated on one's staircase.
My scout was a small friendly individual called Tom. He
would also, of course, bring supper if one ordered it. But
if I remember correctly, one was expected to dine in Hall
four times a week. At any rate one had to pay for it.
Though, however, a lot of one's meals were brought to one
by the relevant scout, I had to cross two quadrangles in

order to get a bath. Life was a curious mixture of ease and austerity. Anyway, I was not only much freer but also much more comfortable than at Marlborough.

Opposite to my abode at the top of a staircase in the New Building at St. John's were the rooms of a young man who came from a school in London and spoke with a pronounced Cockney accent. He had obtained a scholarship and, to his credit, was a very hard worker, evidently intent on making the most of his opportunities. I do not think that he ever entertained. Presumably his parents were poor and his means very limited. He kept rather to himself and was perfectly harmless. This, however, did not prevent certain 'hearties' or athletic types from raiding his rooms on occasions such as 'Bump Suppers,'* when they had had more than usual to drink. I thought their conduct revolting. But I suppose that as the usual targets of Oxford 'hearties' at the time were the 'aesthetes,' and as St. John's did not have any conspicuous aesthetes, the hearties had to find an outlet for their post-drinking energies in raiding the rooms of inoffensive people such as the Cockney youth. At other times the hearties were pleasant enough, of course.

On one festive occasion in the College a small group of hearties had come up in the course of their post-prandial peregrinations with the intention of wrecking the poor Cockney's rooms. But he had not only 'sported his oak'** but had also put a notice on it saying that he was engaged or just about to be engaged in university examinations and begging to be left in peace. Frustrated, the hearties tried the door opposite. This happened to be mine. Not having anticipated any such visitation, I had left it unlocked as usual. In the hearties trooped, and I

---

* Bump Supper: a supper given to celebrate the making of a 'bump,' i.e., the impact of the stem of a boat against the stern or side of another boat in front of it; in boat-racing at the English Universities, the making of a 'bump' is the technical proof of one boat's overtaking and beating another.

** sport the oak: Univ. colloq. to shut the outer door of one's room as a sign that one is engaged.

welcomed them with what grace I could muster. I thought all would be well. But one of my visitors was a Catholic, a former pupil of a Jesuit Public School. He said something like 'here's a Papist, let's wreck his rooms instead.' Happily there was an Old Marlburian in the group, who vouched for me and led the others away. Not unnaturally, I said to myself, 'so the old school tie is a more effective link than membership of the same Church.'

In the rooms underneath me there lived a young man whose name I have entirely forgotten. He was somewhat odd. One day, when I was passing by, he invited me into his living-room. He then disappeared into his bedroom. I could hear him cleaning his teeth, but as he showed no sign of emerging, I eventually left. The youth fell victim to religious mania and had to be removed to a hospital. I seem to recollect that he gashed himself with a knife. Anyway, he disappeared into the care of the doctors.

As I have already mentioned, John Parker, with whom I had shared a study for a while at Marlborough, was also an undergraduate at St. John's. But when I went into digs (as at that time one had to after two years in College) we saw little of one another. As a recent and fervent convert, I was interested in meeting some fellow Catholics, and my friends tended to be in other Colleges. Next door at Balliol there was Charles Dessain, who later became an Oratorian at Birmingham and worked assiduously at editing Newman's letters. Also at Balliol was a Spanish undergraduate, Lucas de Oriol, who came from a very wealthy and profoundly Catholic family and with whom I stayed for some three weeks at Las Arenas near Bilbao in the summer vacation of 1928. Another friend at Balliol was Gervase Mathew, who became a Dominican and later lectured on Byzantine studies at Oxford. As far as I can remember, James Woodroffe was also at Balliol, for I am pretty sure that on more than one occasion he treated me to iced coffee on the lawn in summer. Anyway, I visted Belgium with him and my brother (also at Balliol) in the course of one summer vacation, and Woodroffe was also with me in the north of Spain as a guest of the De Oriol family. At Magdalen there was Frederick Sillem, who later joined the Benedictine Order and is still, at the time of writing, Abbot of Quarr Abbey in the Isle of Wight. Other Catholic friends included, Edmund Howard, who afterwards entered the diplomatic service. His father was for a time British Ambassador in Washington. Then there were Reggies Ellison, who became a lawyer, and Alessandro D'Entrèves, then a postgraduate student, who later was appointed Serena Professor of Italian Studies at Oxford. I remember too Geoffrey de Freitas. I regret that I never met him again after Oxford days. I seem to remember his suggesting a meeting, but for some reason or other I never pursued the matter.

Though he was not a member of the university I should like to say a little about a rather strange character whose name I shall omit. He was a convert to Catholicism who had become a novice under Father Benedict Williamson, a writer of books on mysticism, who was trying to revive the Bridgettine Order for men in England. The venture came to nothing. Father Benedict's idea of how monks should behave seems to have been impossibly austere, and he was left, as far as I am aware, as the only English Bridgettine priest. He went to live in Rome. His ex-novice became a 'Tertiary' of St. Francis and lived in the Capuchin house at Oxford, where he did various jobs. Sometimes he appeared on the streets in a religious habit, looking demure and with his eyes cast down, while at other times he dressed in lay clothes and was anything but demure. It must have been during a visit to the Capuchin house, which was presided over by Father Cuthbert, author of a well known book on St. Francis of Assisi, that I met the ex-novice. He evidently took a fancy to me. Apparently, he had no money at his disposal, and he frequently came to a meal in my rooms or asked me to take him to a cinema. Altogether he took up a great deal of my time. Occasionally he suggested that if he was interfering with my studies, I should tell him so. And this is, indeed, what I should have done. It is possible that as I did not find the textual study of the classics for Honour Moderations at all congenial, I used his importunities as an excuse for failing to give anything like the requisite time to my studies. I was never an ardent classicist, but it is not the least surprising that in Honour Moderations I only achieved a Third. While not particularly concerned about the Greek and Latin texts, I was unjust to my father.

The former novice was a strong Labour supporter. When the General Strike developed and many undergraduates lent a hand with maintaining public services of one kind or another, he urged me not to join the 'strike-breakers'. I was certainly not altogether convinced by his arguments, but I procrastinated, and when at last I made an approach to the railway people, I found that they were not taking on any further volunteers.

After he had left Oxford, I never saw him again, though we occasionally exchanged letters at Christmas. I learned in this way that he was living with a friend in a certain provincial city. He later married and was employed in a Food Office during the early part of the second world war. One day I heard that he had committed suicide. Having sent his wife out shopping, he then gassed himself, having affixed a note to the door of the apartment, telling his wife not to enter but to go for the police. I was told that he had made himself unpopular in the office by complaining about the fiddling which was going on, and that the hostility shown him had preyed on his mind and led to a breakdown. I dare say that some such state of affairs contributed to bringing about his suicide, but I very much doubt whether it was the only cause or even the main one. Not long after his death I had occasion to visit the city where he had worked, as I had undertaken to say Mass for and hear the confessions of German Catholics in a local prisoner of war camp. His widow came to see me. She was evidently a worthy lady and a good Catholic. It became clear that he had made a great mistake in marrying her. Indeed, I doubt whether he should have married at all. In retrospect I can see his inclinations lay in another direction. A talk with the friend with whom he had lived before his marriage pretty well confirmed my reading of the situation. He was genuinely religious and had a lively conscience. I am convinced that he came to find himself in a situation from which he could see no satisfactory egress. Being reduced to a state of utter depression he took his own life, solving his problems by eliminating at one fell swoop the premises which gave rise to the problems. By saying this I am not attempting to offer a moral defence of suicide. I am speaking in terms of a human situation. It seemed that it had become a question of either his wife or himself. The coroner's verdict was one of suicide while of unsound mind, and he was given a Catholic funeral.

When I went up to Oxford, I thought that I should make some contribution at any rate to the sporting activities of the College. Having no enthusiasm for the organized games which had flourished at Marlborough, I decided to take up rowing. In 'Toggers' I rowed as stroke and we did not do so badly. The following year I was in the second Eight. This was pretty disastrous. Rowing was not very popular in the College. In the year when I rowed in the second Eight there were only sixteen rowing men in the College. In other words, there was no spare man. The first Eight was an excellent crew and, if I remember correctly, made a bump every evening. The second Eight, however, was nothing to write home about, and we made a dismal showing in Eights Week. On the last night those in charge of rowing, despairing of our efforts, substituted for the crew a gang of Rugger toughs on the off-chance of their making a bump in the first few minutes of the race. The Rugger men started off with great élan, but to the amusement of the evicted oarsmen they sank before rounding the 'Gut.' So much for that experiment. Unfortunately some relatives had chosen the last day of Eights Week to come and see me row. It was some comfort to see the substitute crew floundering in the river, but the situation was a bit embarrassing all the same. However, thanks to the first Eight there was a Bump Supper in Hall, and I doubtless enjoyed it, in spite of jocular remarks about the shortcomings of the Second Eight.

There have, of course, been stalwart heroes who have succeeded in combining rowing with assiduous study. I was not one of them. After an afternoon on the river I tended to flop into an armchair, eat quantities of hot buttered toast and read some entertaining book. It was not only weakness in resisting the time-wasting visits of the ex-novice which had a detrimental effect on my studies. Rowing was another factor. So when in due course I moved out of College into digs, I extricated myself from the band of oarsmen. The undergraduate in charge of rowing was not at all pleased, not because my services were of any high intrinsic value but because there were so few rowing men in the College. However, I stuck to my resolution. Punting, of course, was another matter. And I remember with pleasure afternoons spent with friends punting up the Cherwell and bathing at Parson's Pleasure.

With rowing successfully abandoned, how did my studies do, i.e., for 'Greats'? Hugh Last, my tutor in Roman history, was a brilliant scholar and a stimulating tutor. When one had finished reading one's essay (during which performance Last might have retired to his bedroom or be standing at his window overlooking St. Giles and syringing his throat), he was accustomed to discourse in an illuminating manner which could hardly fail to arouse some interest. But though I appreciated his services, I did not do him much credit. My interest in Greek and Roman history was limited.

As for philosophy, this was a time when discussion about duty and interest, good and obligation, was ardently pursued at Oxford. I found a lot of it tiresome. It seemed clear enough to me that the concept of good was the basic ethical concept, and that obligation was subordinate. The emotive theory of ethics had not yet really impinged on the Oxford consciousness, but the theory has for me a certain interest. This may be because it seems to express a very real aspect of man's moral life, even if it does so in a markedly one-sided and restricted manner. Anyway, in my time as an undergraduate it was the views of moral philosophers such as H.W.B. Joseph, H.A.

Prichard, E.F. Carritt and W.D. Ross which were being discussed at Oxford; Alfred Ayer had not yet launched *Language, Truth and Logic* (1936), on the shocked circle of older philosophers.

My interest in philosophy was really aroused only when I came to study some metaphysics and came across what I then believed was the Hegelian philosophy. During the summer vacation of my third year at Oxford I felt impelled to write an essay which, on my return to Oxford, I showed to J.D. Mabbott, my philosophy tutor at St. John's. I did not retain the text after my Oxford days, nor have I any clear memory of its contents. But I think that it was inspired more by the thought of Samuel Alexander than by Hegelianism. In any case Mabbott was encouraging, and I began to do more work, though it was admittedly rather late in the day. In the end I managed to pull off a decent Second in Greats, which was some consolation to my father.

My interest in philosophical thought thus began to appear only in or just before my final year at Oxford. What I was interested in was clearly metaphysics understood as directed to the interpretation of Reality with a capital letter. Of Hegel I really knew very little, but I was doubtless impressed and attracted by the comprehensive sweep of his thought. I suppose that I must have hankered after a higher wisdom, after the light that never was on land or sea. This may, indeed, seem odd in a fairly recent and still ardent convert, as, indeed, some friends remarked. In the course of time I have become very much less optimistic in regard to philosophy's competence to deliver the goods, and my respect for more plebeian types of philosophizing has grown. But I can still feel to some extent the attraction of the great world-views or metaphysical visions of reality, even if I am inclined to regard them as historically conditioned perspectives.

It may have been at the end of my first year at Oxford that my brother and I went to northern France for a fortnight. Neither of us had been out of the country before. In fact, it was rather a case of two innocents abroad. At the time the franc stood at about 250 to the

pound, and at Rouen we found accommodation at a very
respectable pension where we were charged only 45
francs *tout compris*, for, that is to say, both room and
meals. We were supposed to be on a walking tour of Normandy, but we naturally wanted to see as much as possible in the time, and after visiting the splendid cathedral
and churches of Rouen, we took train for Paris. We
asked for the cheapest tickets, and in view of our modest
resources we were dismayed to find that we had been
given first-class tickets. Anyway, we arrived in Paris,
went to the Place de la Concorde and naively asked a
gendarme to direct us to a hotel in the centre of the city
where we could put up for 45 francs *tout compris*. Well,
we were sent to a clean and very decent hotel, where we
got rooms for about forty francs each, though without
meals. So we ate out in very modest and cheap places.
Outside the Opera, where we booked seats for a performance of Aida, we allowed ourselves, in our inexperience,
to be persuaded by a tout to buy what he described as
very good places, but which turned out to afford either no
view of the stage or a very restricted one. One evening
we went to the Folies Bergères, where, my brother in-
forms me, I kept my eyes shut most of the time. Notre
Dame, the Sainte Chapelle, the Louvre, Versailles, were
more to my taste.

From Paris we made an expedition to Chartres. At
the Paris station a kindly workman standing behind us in
the queue for tickets drew our attention to the fact that
the clerk had pocketed most of the change from the fairly
high-denomination note which we had offered. But we
were too shy and too mistrustful of our French to make
the fuss which was required, and we suffered the loss in
sorrow. However, we were properly impressed by the
great cathedral of Chartres and its magnificent glass.

After visiting such places as Mont St. Michel,
Bayeux, Caen and doing at any rate a spot of walking in
the pleasant Normandy countryside, we eventually arrived back in England with precious little money left and
no high opinion of French honesty. But we had seen a
good deal, and I remember with pleasure the occasions on

which, when doing some walking, we stopped off in some wayside café for a very cheap cup of good coffee, accompanied by a glass of brandy or Calvados.

One summer vacation James Woodroffe and I visited Belgium for a couple of weeks, enjoying such places at Bruges which were far less crowded than they are now. It was certainly in the summer vacation of 1928 that Woodroffe and I made our visit to Spain, at the invitation of Lucas de Oriol, to stay with him and his family on the sea near Bilbao. My brother had also been invited, but my father would not permit his accepting the invitation. Probably my father was apprehensive that Ernest might follow me into the Catholic Church. An unlikely event, I think, but there it was. So Jamie and I set off for Spain, spending a night or two in Paris on the way. I remember that for some reason or other (perhaps Jamie was having a snooze) I visited a gallery by myself. While admiring a statue by Maillol, I was accosted by a Spanish gentleman who pressed me to have lunch with him. Happily I had the good sense to make excuses, though this was probably more an expression of shyness at talking to strangers than of a real grasp of the situation.

After the lengthy journey from Paris, Jamie and I were met by Lucas de Oriol at San Sebastian and driven along the coast to Las Arenas. Needless to say, we were made very welcome, taken to a couple of bullfights (which did not afford me any pleasure), treated to fishing from the family's yacht in the Bay of Biscay (I disgraced myself by sea-sickness) and shown some historic sites such as Covadonga and Loyola. At Loyola, home of St. Ignatius Loyola, founder of the Jesuit Order, Lucas de Oriol hazarded the prophecy that I would one day become a Jesuit. I did not expect this at the time, but the prophecy was in fact fulfilled.

I am ashamed to say that through my folly the visit to Spain was not a success. Having made what seemed to me friendly jokes about Spanish achievements, I repeated the offence without noticing the resentment and displeasure caused by this behaviour. When at last I understood the state of affairs, it was too late to repair the

damage. My hosts got the impression that I despised
Spain, and a cloud gradually spread over the visit. Jamie
Woodroffe did not seem to me quite to realize what had
happened, but, of course, he was not responsible for the
situation.

At that time General Primo de Rivera was still governing Spain as what amounted to a dictator, and King
Alfonso XIII was still on the throne. The Spanish Civil
War lay in the future. It was not in fact very far away,
but I do not recall any talk about politics or social problems. If there was, I have forgotten it. Later on the De
Oriol family, which owned steel mines at Bilbao, adhered
to the cause of General Franco. At any rate one De Oriol
brother was killed fighting in the Civil War, and another
held some important position in the Franco government,
unless my memory fails me. But in that far away summer the horrors of the Civil War lay in the future, and,
as far as I was concerned, the only blot on those sun-
drenched weeks was my own silly conduct and its conse-
quences, a very minor incident compared with the historical events in store.

As I have mentioned, my brother Ernest was not allowed to accompany me to Spain. Curiously, however, my
father had not objected to our responding to an advertisement in a newspaper which said that during the summer
vacation accommodation would be available in a villa up
behind Menton on the French Riviera. As a result of inquiry we discovered that we could live there quite
cheaply. With our parents' agreement, therefore (I think
that mother had persuaded father to let the boys take the
risk) Ernest and I had arranged to meet in the south of
France. When the Spanish visit came to an end James
Woodroffe and I travelled to Bayonne, where James told
the taxi-driver to take us to "the best hotel in the town."
I felt that this lordly gesture was all very well for a man
who was on his way back to England, but a different
matter for me who would have further expenses abroad.
However, the hotel was certainly comfortable.

Ernest and I met at Nice and we went on together to
Menton, where we were then faced with the task of find-

ing the villa where we were to stay. A taxi took us up into the hills behind the town, but the driver could not possibly get his machine down the path through the olive groves to the villa. Or so he said. Anyway he set us and our baggage down by the roadside. Neither the driver nor we had the necessary change, but a passing priest kindly solved the problem. We had with us a trunk, with a good many books, as we optimistically had it in mind to do a good deal of reading for the university papers. However, in the end we arrived, plus baggage, at the villa, only to find that the owner, who had put the advertisement in the paper, had gone off with someone else's husband to England. But all was well. A lady named Mrs. Ingold was installed and would look after us.

The villa (to dignify the erection with this title) had its attractions. True, it was not quite what we had imagined after reading the description in the advertisement. But it was pleasant to dine outside in the evening and to hear little but the constant chirping of the cicadas and the occasional barking of a dog. However, the idyllic scene was somewhat marred by the presence of fearsome hornets, attracted by the oil lamp on the table. Further, the villa was a very considerable distance from the sea, and as the return journey was a constant steep ascent through the olive groves, the refreshing effects of a bathe had entirely disappeared by the time we got back. It was no matter for surprise that Mrs. Ingold soon tired of country life and invited us to stay in her flat in Menton. So after a week at the country villa we all three migrated down to Menton. I suppose that there should have been a renegotiation of contract. Indeed, Mrs. Ingold's mother used to give strong hints from time to time that this was the case. But Ernest and I had come to Menton on the understanding that we would pay a certain sum for our summer stay, and we took no notice of the hints. (Mrs. Ingold herself never made any.) Perhaps it was just as well. For when we arrived back at Taunton after a month at Menton, we had about one and sixpence between us.

In those days there were practically no tourists in the summer. Most of the hotels were shut. The staffs either transferred to hotels on the north coast or found other work. My brother and I thus had the beach pretty well to ourselves, and we spent hours there, bathing and lying in the sun, retiring now and again to a cafe for an ice or a drink. I remember trying to study Aristotle's *Ethics*, but the environment was not conducive to serious study. At midday we went back to the flat for an abundant repast, after which we had to have a siesta. Then back to the sea. After supper we generally went with Mrs. Ingold to sit in the Cafe Glacier. Acquaintances of our hostess speculated about which of us was living with her. The answer was that neither of us was. My brother and I had our beds in the same room, where we slept under mosquito nets, hoping that the troublesome insects would not succeed in penetrating our protection.

One young lady who lived at Menton and who had heard that two Oxford undergraduates were coming for a month expected to have the time of her life. Poor girl, she soon discovered her mistake. We never sought her out. Nor indeed did we ever invite any of the girls in the Cafe Glacier to dance. Apart from our natural reserve and my own ethico-religious preoccupations, we were in any case pretty impecunious. Enjoying the meals provided by Mrs. Ingold and our frequent dips in the Mediterranean were more in our line than flirtation. We made few expeditions, though I remember our visiting Sospel in the Alpes Maritimes and also Bordighera, where we had a grand time diving off a rock into clear warm water.

During the summer months the far from well-heeled foreign residents, who were nobodies in the winter season, came into their own. I remember an odd Englishman, a travel agent I think, who was pursuing our hostess. While we were up at the villa in the hills during the first part of our stay at Menton, he would arrive in the morning, lie down on a sofa and read a novel, getting up only for meals. One day, when we were already installed in Mrs. Ingold's flat in town, the good man invited us all to accompany him one evening to Monte Carlo in his ramshackle car. In the square opposite the Casino he ordered drinks for the company. But immediately he saw the waiter approaching with the bill, he recognized someone he knew on the other side of the square and did not return until the account had been settled. On the way back to Menton he was obviously annoyed that no progress had been made in his courtship of our hostess (her husband was apparently in Switzerland) and he started to drive in a way calculated to scare the wits out of Mrs. Ingold, not so much on her own account as on that of her six-year old daughter. The mother imagined the windscreen shattering in an accident and the girl's face being disfigured by flying glass. Her pleas had no effect on the driver; on the contrary. So my brother and I had to tell him sharply to stop playing the fool, and his behaviour then improved.

What with three weeks in Spain and a month on the French Riviera, the summer vacation of 1928 passed very pleasantly, and I returned to Oxford with a mind to do some real work for Greats during my final year at the university. At this time I was living in digs off the Iffley Road, sharing a sitting-room with a worthy Catholic undergraduate from the north of England. I remember that on one occasion our landlady had bought some cheese for us in the market. When the cheese was cut, out jumped a host of lively maggots. Being put off by this spectacle I hid the offending article behind the aspidistra. When the landlady came in and failed to see her cheese, she trotted round the room in search of it. A trivial incident; but it is so often trivial incidents which for some reason or other stick in one's memory. Thus I remember clearly that my bedroom was extremely cold in winter and that on rising I had to thaw out my sponge. One night I woke up to hear what I thought was someone jumping in through the window. I sprang out of bed, prepared to do battle with the intruder; but I discovered that it was only a large cat which had climbed up onto a penthouse outside and leaped in through the open window.

While I was living in digs, I made good use of the Oxford Union for purposes of reading and study, but I never spoke in a debate and rarely went to one. However, I remember taking a Canadian priest as a guest to a debate at which King George of the Hellenes was to be a principal speaker. The king was then enduring one of his periods of exile, and he had consented to speak in defence of the Public Schools. When the officers of the Union and the principal speakers entered the debating hall after their dinner, my guest was extremely shocked to see the president of the Union taking his place on the elevated chair which he imagined to have been reserved for King George. I pointed out to him that it was only normal procedure which was being followed and that it would be very odd if one of the invited speakers were to usurp the president's official place. All to no avail. My guest remained convinced that deliberate disrespect had been shown to Royalty. King George himself was presumably perfectly well aware that no such disrespect was intended.

As is obvious to any reader, my life at Oxford was pretty tame. It bore little resemblance to the life depicted in, for example, the diaries of Evelyn Waugh. Apart from the means to lead such a life, I also lacked the inclination to do so. This was not, I regret to say, because of devotion to my studies. As I have related, it was not until my final year that any real interest in them manifested itself, and then it was simply an interest in metaphysical speculation. My dominant interest lay partly in exploring the new world which I had entered through my reception into the Catholic Church while still at Marlborough and partly in religious mysticism. Still, as I have noted, I obtained a decent Second in *Literae Humaniores*, and this brought my undistinguished career at Oxford to a close, apart, of course, from taking the steps to proceed, at the appropriate times, B.A. and then M.A., Oxon.

Chapter 5

Joining the Jesuits

LIKE MOST SMALL BOYS, I SUPPOSE, I HAD PASSING DREAMS of what I might be in the future, whether driver of an express train or explorer or an ambassador for one's country. But my more basic and abiding intention was that of entering the Church, as it is sometimes oddly expressed, as though the Church were identical with its ordained members. It was arguably natural enough that I should think along this line. After all, two of my uncles were Anglican bishops, and though my father had been a judge, not a clergyman, he was the son of one, and he took an active part in the life of the Church of England at various levels. To be sure, I entertained a much more exalted concept of the status and functions of a priest than was usual in the kind of Anglicanism in which I was brought up; but this does not alter the fact that there was a good deal in my upbringing to suggest to me the idea of the priesthood.

Obviously, as far as logical possibility is concerned, I might have reacted strongly against this upbringing. And to a certain extent I did. But the reaction was directed more against the brand of Anglicanism with which I was primarily acquainted, at home and at school; and during my teens this reaction took the form of a powerful attraction towards Catholicism. When, however, I had become

Catholic, I do not think that I had any other really serious aspiration in my mind than that of being ordained a
priest. In this respect there was continuity. It is true
that during the difficult time following my reception into
the Catholic Church I had fleeting thoughts of becoming a
schoolmaster. For I realized, of course, that while my
being a Catholic was a source of sorrow and disappointment to my father, ordination to the Catholic priesthood
would be even more obnoxious to him. Sometimes I had
been attracted by the idea of seeking admission to the
foreign service; but at the time this would require money,
and I could hardly expect my father to welcome and
further the project. Schoolmastering was a much more
practicable proposition. I do not think, however, that the
idea of becoming a lay schoolmaster was ever much more
than a passing thought. It was never in serious competi-
tion with the idea of becoming a priest.

What sort of a priest? The priests at Taunton, first
Canon O'Shaugnessy and than Canon Iles, belonged to the
diocese of Clifton, and though Father Louis Valluet, who
received me into the Catholic Church, was a member of a
religious Congregation (Missionaries of St. Francis de
Sales), he worked in the Clifton diocese as parish priest of
Devizes. It was not unnatural therefore that when I went
down from Oxford I should offer myself to the diocese of
Clifton as a candidate for the diocesan priesthood. I was
accepted by that somewhat eccentric old gentleman Bishop
George Ambrose Burton. Dr. Burton was a scholar, a great
reader of the classics, especially Virgil whose poetry he
seemed to know by heart in its entirety. The story was
that he sat up in his house at Leigh Woods reading the
classics and refusing to have a telephone installed so that
his studies could not be interrupted by phone calls from
the diocesan clergy. He could be an eloquent preacher, but
in Rome he had picked up the habit of taking snuff, even
in the pupit, and I remember that when, as a boy, I heard
him preach at Taunton on the occasion of a confirmation I
thought that he was a bad-mannered old fellow who had
left his handkerchief behind. He once wrote a long Pasto-
ral Letter to his flock in which he criticized Father de la

Taille's theory of the essence of the sacrifice of the Mass and defended the theological theory which he himself favoured. How much of what he wrote was understood by the Catholics of Gloucestershire, Wiltshire and Somerset, when it was duly read to them by their parish clergy, is open to question. Very little, I imagine.

However this may be, Bishop Burton arranged for me to go to the English College in Rome, the students of which attend the Gregorian University (run by the Jesuits) for their ecclesiastical studies. As, however, my father was at this time involved in some distress of mind which was unconnected with my own religious doings or misdoings, I thought that I ought not to make things more difficult for him by departing for Rome. This may sound odd, but in those days the students of the English College in Rome did not normally visit England again until they had completed the first three years of their studies at the Gregorian University, whereas, if I were studying at a seminary in England, I could go home for the vacations. So I approached the bishop, and he made arrangements for me to go to Oscott College near Birmingham.

At that time at Oscott students slept in cubicles in dormitories and studied downstairs, where the junior students at any rate were grouped in threes. I was allocated to a room in which one of the group was a Plymouth Brother who had been converted to Catholicism. As far as I could see, he was still a Plymouth Brother to all intents and purposes, and I was not surprised to hear later on that he had returned to his native fold.

For the first two of the six years course the students had to study philosophy. The philosophy lecturer in the first year had been a parish priest and had been brought to Oscott by the Archbishop of Birmingham to teach plainchant. Music was his strong point. He did not remember much of whatever philosophy he had once learned, and I doubt whether he had much interest in the subject. It was sometimes quite evident that lectures had not been prepared, and I remember that on one occasion the good man read us a story by Anatole France instead.

At the time all the writings of Anatole France were on the Index of prohibited books. But if the lecturer was aware of this fact, it did not bother him. A refreshing incident, I thought.

It could hardly be claimed successfully that my studies at Oxford had been either extensive or profound. But I had at any rate picked up something, and on one occasion I visited the first year lecturer in philosophy in his room and put some logical problems to him. His way of coping with the situation was to tell me to put all that Oxford stuff out of my head and give my attention to Scholastic truth. At the time I was not favourably impressed by this attitude, but nowadays I rather sympathize with the good priest. The majority of candidates for the priesthood are obviously not budding philosophers; they have other aims in mind. What philosophical studies they are deemed to require are inevitably tailored to their needs and are likely to have a predominantly apologetic slant. As for the lecturers in seminaries, in most cases they put in some years teaching philosophy, treated as religious apologetics for the most part, and then escaped to parishes, where their hearts generally lay. It is true that nowadays much more is expected of the lecturers in seminaries, and standards have certainly risen. Among teachers of philosophy in ecclesiastical seminaries one can undoubtedly encounter serious thinkers, who are well acquainted with modern philosophical thought and who are quite prepared to grapple with relevant problems. But my reminiscences go back, of course, to a time when philosophical questioning on the part of teachers and pupils was not exactly encouraged.

In the case of Scripture we were much better off. Our lecturer at Oscott was Dr. Bird, who had published a work on the Psalms and who was a hard worker and a forceful and lively lecturer. If I remember correctly, there was a five-year cycle in Biblical studies. In my year at Oscott Dr. Bird took us through the book of *Jonas*, among other parts of the Bible. He was very careful what he said about Jonas and outlined a number of different lines of interpretation; but it was pretty clear that he himself regarded the book as a story designed to drive home a moral lesson. Distinguishing between various literary forms, historical narrative, moral tale and so on is now, of course, a commonplace among Catholic biblical scholars. It is taken for granted, but at the time when I studied for a year at Oscott a seminary lecturer had to be very circumspect, if he wished to retain his job. Dr. Bird also taught us Hebrew, but I cannot say that I have remembered much of what I learned. The general practice was to get up enough to pass the examination and then to forget it.

Among those of my fellow students whom I got to know fairly well and with whom I went for walks were Robert Woodbridge, who was ordained for the Nottingham diocese, Ethelbert Payne, who became a Canon in the Northampton diocese, and Richard Foster, who was to become a Scripture scholar and in time Rector of Oscott College. I remember academic discussions with Dick Foster, and I recollect a visit to Belgium with Bob Woodbridge and my brother after the end of my year at Oscott. The Rector of the College during my sojourn there was Monsignor Dey, later Roman Catholic Bishop for the armed forces. He was responsible for some modifications in the traditional rather rigid discipline of the College. For example, he permitted students to go for walks alone, if they so wished. I had the impression that the Vice-Rector, Dr. Bird, did not altogether approve of all the reforms instituted by the Rector, but they were bound to come in time.

At this point I must retrace my steps and refer again to my four years at Oxford. While at the university, I considered the possibility of joining a religious order. In some cases I had simply read a life of the founder of the order in question or of some saint who had belonged to it. This was hardly an adequate guide to what membership of the relevant order would actually be like or involve. For a time I felt some attraction to the Carthusians, and I visited their monastery at Parkminster in Sussex once or twice for some days and thus had some idea at any rate of the monks' cloistered and austere lives. Looking back, however, I can see that the Charterhouse would certainly not have suited me. In any case my inability to sing would have disqualified me. The long services are unaccompanied by any organ, and 'no voice, no vocation' is a firm rule. I knew an archbishop (now dead) who in his earlier days entered the Charterhouse in Sussex but was not permitted to take his vows, as he could not sing a note, a fact which became obvious to all who later on heard his attempts to celebrate High Mass.

At Oxford I soon got to know the Jesuits, both at Campion Hall and at the parish of St. Aloysius, which was then run by the Jesuits. They were very kind to me, and I often dined at Campion Hall on Sundays after attending the short Benediction service. It rather embarrassed me to go there to Benediction, as I imagined that it might be thought that I was expecting to stop to dinner. I would therefore try to escape directly the short service was over. But the Master, Father Vignaux, doubtless guessing my fears, often sent a member of the Community to arrest my flight and invite me in to dinner. On Thursdays in term, when I was not otherwise engaged, I often took a walk with Father J.P. O'Donohoe, who talked about literature, and then had tea at Campion Hall. From time to time I invited some member of the Community to a meal in my rooms at St. John's or to my lodgings when I was living out of College.

The friendliness of the Jesuits to a raw convert doubtless influenced me more than I realized at the time. In spite, however, of frequent contacts with members of the order, I do not recollect a single occasion on which any Jesuit suggested that I should apply to join the Society of Jesus. I remember a priest of another order urging me *not* to think of the Jesuits but to join the order to which he himself belonged. But no Jesuit acted in this sort of way. In point of fact when someone applies to join the Society of Jesus, one of the questions put to him is whether any pressure was brought to bear on him by any member of the order. And in the past at any rate this has not infrequently been understood by individual Jesuits as implying that even if a young man is wondering whether he should join a religious order or congregation or aim at becoming a diocesan priest, no positive suggestion should ever be made that he might ask himself whether life in the Society of Jesus might not possibly be the sort of thing for which he was looking. There is a considerable difference between bringing pressure to bear on someone and simply suggesting a possibility worth considering for this or that reason. However this may be, I do not remember any Jesuit suggesting to me that I should apply for admission to the order, much less bringing any pressure to bear.

Anyway, during the course of my year at Oscott my mind moved in the direction of the Jesuits, and when Archbishop Goodier, a Jesuit who had been a predecessor of Archbishop Roberts in the see of Bombay, came to the College to conduct the annual spiritual retreat for the students, I sought him out privately, told him of my wish to become a Jesuit and asked his advice. He advised me to make a retreat in the Jesuit novitiate at Roehampton, so that I could have some idea at least of what I was proposing to let myself in for. When I informed Monsignor Dey that I intended to apply for admission to the Society of Jesus, he remarked that this was precisely what he had been afraid of all along. However this may be, when the first year of my studies at Oscott was over, I made a retreat at Roehampton under the direction of Father Peers Smith and then made a formal request to the Jesuit Provincial, Father Henry Keane, for admission as a novice of the order. After I had had the customary interviews with several Jesuit Fathers appointed for the purpose, the Provincial wrote to tell me that I would be accepted as a novice and was to present myself at the noviceship on the 7th of September, 1930.

Until I had received this letter of acceptance from the Provincial, I had told my parents nothing of what was in my mind, nothing definite at any rate. I have indeed the excuse that as my becoming a Jesuit would be an additional blow for my father I did not want to cause him avoidable distress by revealing my intention when there was still the possibility that the Jesuit authorities would not accept me. At the same time I feel sure that my dislike for argument and tension played a large part in determining my conduct. If one has really made up one's mind what one proposes to do, it saves one a lot of trouble if one simply presents people with an accomplished fact. Though, however, my conduct seems to me understandable, I do not consider it admirable. My father thought of the Catholic Church as un-English, foreign, unsuited for an English gentleman, and he would be likely to regard the Jesuits as even more un-English than Catholics in general. To spring it on him that I was shortly going to leave home to join the notorious order in question can reasonably be described as unfeeling or callous. All the same, I retain the uneasy feeling that I should have acted otherwise than I did.

When the time came to take the train from Taunton to London, I felt, and I think that other members of the family also felt, a very much greater sense of parting than when I left for Oscott College. And with justification. At Oscott there were vacations during which the students lived at home with their families; and if I eventually became a priest in the diocese of Clifton, it would have been easy to see my parents fairly often. Further, though a diocesan priest's annual holidays are by no means long and depend on his success in finding someone to hold the fort in his absence, he can spend them where he likes. With the Jesuits, however, the situation was very different. At the time of which I am writing members of the order did not return home unless a parent was very seriously ill. Relatives could indeed pay occasional and brief visits to the Jesuit, but he could go to stay at home only after his ordination to the priesthood (for five nights) and, if he were to be sent on a foreign mission, for some days before his departure. In practice, of course, the situation was milder than this. Once a Jesuit had been ordained and had finished his studies, he could try to arrange to 'supply' for a while during the holidays of a priest in his home town or in the vicinity. Thus as a priest I regularly went to Taunton on this basis while my mother (who long outlived my father) was still alive. One slept in the priest's house, but apart from the daily morning Mass and the rather heavy weekends one was free to spend most of the time with one's family, as a supply priest's duties are generally kept to the minimum necessary. When, however, I left for the noviceship at Roehampton, ordination lay a long way ahead. In the Society of Jesus there was a jocular saying that for a Jesuit, ordination was a reward for a well-spent life. This may have been somewhat of an exaggeration, but the period of preparation or training was at the time exceptionally long. So when I parted from my parents and brother at Taunton station and the London express pulled out, I felt that it was to all intents and purposes goodbye to the old life.

This was, of course, precisely what it was intended to be, in accordance with the Gospel idea of leaving father and mother to follow Christ. It seems to me, however, that in my case at any rate there was too little, rather than too much, thought for the family. In point of fact the situation was greatly changed by the second World War. In view of such factors as bombing raids, which threatened the lives of the civilian population, the Jesuit Provincial gave leave pretty freely to Jesuit students or 'scholastics' to visit their families at reasonable intervals. Once the practice had been modified, it obviously became much easier to recognize the truth that even Jesuits have duties to their families. The traditions of the Society of Jesus, going back to its heroic origins, governed the minds of its Superiors for centuries and led them to place a rather one-sided emphasis on the ideal of leaving all, including one's family, to follow Christ. Changes in external circumstances made it easier to perceive other aspects of the situation. This is a pattern which tends to recur. For example, when people had become used to living in a pluralist society, they could see for themselves that religious uniformity was by no means required for social cohesion, and it became easier to understand the iniquity of the religious persecutions which were once such a terrible blot on the life of Christian Europe. By saying this I do not intend to belittle, much less to reject, the ideals upheld by Christ. But one should bear in mind the danger of self-deception. Thus it is possible to gloss over callous and unfeeling conduct to others, say members of one's family, as exemplifying the abandonment of earthly ties for the sake of following Christ. It is not, I think, a question of strictness and fidelity degenerating into laxity and self-indulgence. One might say that it is a matter of coming to see more clearly that the pursuit of Christian ideals does not free one from obligations imposed by basic 'natural law.' Or one might say that it is a question of not allowing oneself to be hypnotized by one single aspect of the Gospel message and thus becoming blind to other relevant aspects.

In the early years of my life in the Society of Jesus I much enjoyed the occasional visits of relatives, and I could still take an interest in matters relating to life down at Taunton. Later on, however, when I had become absorbed in the academic life of teaching and writing, I experienced a sense of discontinuity of interest which tended to make my visits to Taunton somewhat trying. My father died when I was still a Jesuit scholastic. I continued, of course to visit my mother every summer (supplying for the parish priest during his holiday or that of his curate), but at the end of the three weeks or so I had the unpleasant feeling of having failed her, of having set out with the determination to bridge a growing gulf and then having failed to do so. My mother doubtless experienced similar feelings. This is probably a common enough phenomenon. But it is perhaps intensified when one is leading an academic and celibate life, remote from the sort of interests which loom large on the mental horizon of most upper middle class people in a provincial town. It is not a question of one being superior to the other. It is more a question of a natural growing apart, of a divergence of interests. The trouble is that this growing apart can cause pain to the people concerned.

To return to the story of my joining the order in the first place. In those days there were many applicants to the Society, and I found myself pitched into a large group of fellow 'probationers,' none of whom I knew. Most of the new novices had come straight from Jesuit schools, especially Stonyhurst College in Lancashire and Mount St. Mary's near Sheffield, though there were some from other Jesuit schools in England or Scotland. Having been at Oxford and having then spent a year at Oscott, I was, of course, older than the novices who had come straight from school. But there were one or two newcomers, converts, who were older than I. Nowadays novices, though much fewer in number, tend to be considerably more mature, having already taken university degrees or had jobs or both. But at the time when I joined the great bulk of the novices were ex-pupils of Jesuit schools and generally not more than eighteen years old. A good many were already acquainted with one another, having been contemporaries at school.

The noviceship lasted two years. Life was simple and uneventful, consisting mainly of regular prayer and meditation, instruction in spirituality and on the nature, ideals and constitutions of the Society of Jesus, of useful duties in the house, such as sweeping, washing up and helping the cook, and of outdoor work in the then extensive grounds and gardens of Manresa House, Roehampton. The life was varied to some extent by weekly games of football for those who wished to play and by walks for those who did not. In those days there was little study of an academic nature in the noviceship. We spent a great deal more time in household chores and in 'outdoor works,' as we called them, than in study. We lived our lives together. On walks, for example, we were generally in companies of threes. The food was excellent and abundant. Regularity and monotony constituted the tests of perseverance rather than any physical hardships.

Novices who had been at Jesuit schools obviously knew some Jesuits and had doubtless been on friendly terms with one or more; but it by no means followed necessarily that they knew much about the order, even if they had chosen to enter the noviceship with a view to testing their vocations. One of the functions of the novitiate was, of course, to initiate them into the mind or spirit of the Society of Jesus. Up to a point our Master of Novices was admirably suited for this task. For he was an exemplary Jesuit priest with the highest ideals and was also both firm and sympathetic. He was extremely accessible, and as he had been a chaplain in the first world war, he was naturally acquainted with a wide range of human types. Though, however, he was rightly respected by his novices, he had a marked inclination to foster among his charges the special devotions which for one reason or another appealed to him, and he referred frequently to the writings of certain pious persons, male and female, who believed that they had messages from on high to communicate. In other words, there was perhaps somewhat too much of a hothouse atmosphere, the real suitability of which as a preparation for the realities of life in the order was at any rate open to discussion. It was noticeable that one or two of those whom the Master of Novices had seemed to regard as model novices did not long persevere in the order once they had completed the noviceship and taken first vows, whereas some of those who had been regarded as too free and easy in their ways subsequently did excellent and solid work as Jesuit priests.

This rather enclosed and piety-centred life was doubtless largely responsible for the infectious fits of giggling which broke out on frequent occasions, though never when the Master of Novices was talking to us. For example, on Sundays novices sometimes assisted at services at the Catholic parish church which adjoined the noviceship grounds. On these occasions we were placed in the stalls up in what one might describe as the choir of the church, at any rate in full view of the congregation. Sometimes the preacher or the celebrant had some odd mannerisms, and I can recollect occasions on which most of us were pretty well convulsed by badly suppressed, and sometimes not suppressed, laughter. The giggling fits were not due to any spirit of irreverence. They were due to what was described as 'strain.' What the congregation thought of these performances I do not know. It must have been an odd sight to see a band of pious novices sitting behind the preacher and laughing their heads off or now and again breaking into fits of giggles. I hasten to add that with the relaxation of tension in modern noviceships the phenomenon in question has, I understand, disappeared. Jesuit novices now lead a much less sequestered and a much more open life.

The two years passed by, and with other second-year novices I took my first vows on the 8th September, 1932, thus exchanging the status of a novice for that of a 'scholastic.' At that time most of the young men who had just completed the noviceship spent one or two further years at Roehampton in what was called the 'Juniorate,' devoting their attention to humanistic studies, while some took the intermediate examinations of the University of London. As I already had a university degree, I was spared the Juniorate and was sent at once, with a group of other recently fledged scholastics, to Heythrop College in Oxfordshire to pursue philosophical studies. These customarily lasted for three years, but in view of my year at Oscott I was placed in the second year. Once again I found myself in the midst of companions whom I had not met before and had thus to break fresh ground.

Chapter 6

Towards Ordination

HEYTHROP COLLEGE IN OXFORDSHIRE STOOD AT A RELA-
tively high altitude on the edge of the Cotswolds, some
four miles from the small market-town of Chipping Nor-
ton. The main block had been the home of the Talbot
family, the Earls of Shrewsbury, and later of the Brassey
family. There had been at least two conflagrations, but
the shell of the eighteenth-century house survived. Before the Jesuits arrived in 1926 they arranged for the addition of two wings, one of which housed the students of
theology, while the students of philosophy were accommo-
dated in the other. Each scholastic had his own room,
where he studied and slept. The staff lived, for the most
part, in the central mansion. The College was approached by a very long drive from the Oxford-Stratford
road, and it had extensive grounds. Besides football and
cricket fields and tennis-courts there was a homemade
golf-course, a swimming-bath, two lakes, woods and a
home-farm. Being right in the country, we could walk for
miles on all sides, and I remember with great pleasure
many delightful rambles and picnics during my years as a
student there. For some tastes, of course, the College was
too remote from city life. Oxford was some sixteen miles
away. But there was plenty of fresh air, and we had
abundant opportunities for enjoying the country-side. As

for numbers, the Jesuit community, including professors, scholastics (studying philosophy or theology as the case might be) and laybrothers was pretty large. I remember that one year the number amounted to 153, which, as pointed out at the time, was that of the fishes mentioned in the twenty-first chapter of St. John's Gospel.

At the time when I became a Jesuit (things are very different today) novices never had a holiday outside the noviceship; they remained at Roehampton for the whole two-year period. At Heythrop College, however, students of philosophy and theology went for successive fortnights in the summer vacation to Barmouth on the Welsh coast, where the English Province had a rather derelict house near the sea. Conditions may have been primitive and crowded in some ways, but most of us found these two weeks by the sea an enjoyable tonic. I well remember climbing Cader Idris, Snowdon and other neighbouring mountains with groups of scholastics, rowing up the river to partake of a communal breakfast at the George, and, of course, bathing frequently in the sea. We were very free, and after a day in the open air we returned with hearty appetites for our excellent evening dinner. To the young Jesuits after the second world war communal holidays at Barmouth were not so congenial. Many preferred to go off on some venture of their own or in small goups. This is quite understandable. Besides, we no longer have the numbers which we had in the old days. But the Barmouth communal holidays were certainly not lacking in all advantages. For one thing, people who had perhaps little contact with one another during the course of the academic year tended to learn to appreciate one another's good points at Barmouth.

The studies at the old Heythrop lasted seven years, three being devoted to philosophy and four to theology. It does not follow, however, that they were pursued continuously throughout. In most cases, when a student had completed the three years of philosophical studies, he was sent to teach for some years in a Jesuit school or to study for a secular degree at Oxford or London, after which he would probably also have to put in a period of teaching before beginning his theological studies. As therefore there was generally a gap of some six or seven years between a Jesuit student's completion of his philosophical studies and the time when he began to study theology, the students of theology tended to be not only older and more mature but also markedly browned off, disinclined, that is to say, to listen to frequent lectures and very critical of their teachers. Further, as ordination to the priesthood normally took place at the end of the third year of theology, students in the fourth and final year of theology were generally already priests and understandably looking forward to the end of the long years of study and to the commencement of a more active life. A few, of course, were genuinely interested in this or that branch of philosophy or theology and hoped to specialize and to have the opportunity of devoting themselves to academic pursuits. It hardly needs saying, however, that most young Jesuits had other things in mind than continuing philosophical or theological studies with a view to lecturing on such subjects, especially when it was a case of addressing hearers whose lively interest in what was being dished out to them could not be simply taken for granted.

In Catholic seminaries the basic programme of ecclesiastical studies was drawn up by the relevant Roman authorities. It was the Congregation of Studies in Rome which settled the matter, not national hierarchies, and still less individual bishops or rectors of seminaries. In the Society of Jesus the demands of the Church were, of course, met, but the Society was by no means content with the minimum requirements for ordination purposes. There was an elaborate and centrally devised programme of studies geared to the taking of Pontifical degrees in philosophy and theology. At the time, however, there was one perhaps rather odd difference between studies in the faculty of philosophy and studies in the faculty of theology. In the case of philosophy all students were deemed to be studying for the degree of Licentiate in Philosophy, a classified honours degree. They did not all obtain the degree, of course; there were those who had little interest in and possibly no real aptitude for real philosophical reflection. But they were none the less committed to three years of study, covering the various traditional branches of philosophy and some associated disciplines such as experimental psychology and biology. It was, however, only those who had attained the required standard in the final examinations in philosophy who were later admitted to what was known as the 'long course' in theology. In point of fact both the 'long' course and the 'short' course lasted for the same period, four years; but in the latter some of the subjects included in the former were omitted. For the matter of that, students who started in the long course but proved unable to reach the required standards in the annual examinations migrated to the short course. In other words, once the philosophical studies were over, a process of sorting out took place, whereas in those days there was one common philosophical programme, which normally at any rate, all Jesuit students of philosophy were expected to follow. Later on this state of affairs underwent change. Well before Heythrop College left its Cotswolds home and migrated to London, matters were so arranged that only those students who had a real interest in and aptitude for philosophy continued their studies for three years. The others covered what was thought to be necessary for the training of a Jesuit priest in two years and then either left Heythrop or began theological studies. This was far better both for students and teachers.

I have already mentioned that in my last year at Oxford I was attracted by what I optimistically believed to be Hegelianism. However, this may be, at Heythrop I became or claimed to have become a Thomist. Hence the philosophical studies were not as uncongenial to me as they might have been. I do not mean that we were prevented from reading anything other than the works of St. Thomas Aquinas. As the Index existed in those days, we had to ask leave to read books condemned by Rome; but there was no particular difficulty in obtaining permission and we were encouraged to make ourselves acquainted with the relevant writings of 'adversaries,' as they were described. As for literary work, I remember studying Bergson and writing an article on his thought, which was published in the American periodical *The Modern School-man*. To be sure, the Jesuit censor insisted on my peppering the article with quotations from St. Thomas Aquinas before I despatched it to America. He doubtless wanted me to show that anything of value in Bergson had been anticipated by Aquinas, an attitude which is much less common nowadays than it used to be. However, the article appeared all right. I also remember writing a Latin article on the theory of substantial forms, which was published in an Italian periodical edited by the Dominican Fathers. The two essays appeared in 1934 and initiated my literary activity.

In view of the fact that I was being thought of as a possible future member of the Heythrop staff, I was not sent out to teach when I had finished my philosophical studies but was directed straight to the study of theology. Once more I found myself among strangers, scholastics who had been considerably longer in the order than I had. But the move certainly pleased me. Schools were often reluctant to release young masters to begin their theological studies and raised objections with the Provincial, so that the period of teaching between philosophy and theology was sometimes unduly prolonged. If during my life as a Jesuit priest I have been able to do a good deal of writing, this was greatly facilitated by the fact that I was able to pursue my ordination studies continuously and to start my activity as a lecturer when I still had a good deal of energy at my disposal.

At that time in the case of theology, as in that of philosophy, teaching was done mainly by lectures, of which there were far too many. After the first two years of theological studies the lecture-load became somewhat lighter, as moral theology and some other subjects had been cleared out of the way. None the less the load was too heavy for men who had already gone through a good many years of study and who, moreover, started the day with an hour and a half's spiritual duties before breakfast. The situation was not improved by the fact that in some cases lecturers kept so closely to their textbooks or to stencilled and already circulated 'codices' that one might just as well have read what they had to say in the privacy of one's room. It was not, however, a question of people being unable to see that the system had any faults; it was much more a question of faithful adherence to a centrally imposed programme, by Rome that is to say.

The trouble was not simply an over-abundance of lectures, with the added difficulty that the medium of teaching was Latin (through some professors took a much looser view than others of what this regulation entailed). Both in philosophy and in systematic or dogmatic theology the material to be covered was divided into a series of 'theses,' students being expected to learn to understand and be prepared to defend by appropriate arguments each successive thesis. The system was not indeed without its virtues or strong points. It certainly provided a good training in clarity and precision of thought, in recognition of needed distinctions, and in argumentation. Further, the fact that the scheme of studies was basically common to all Jesuit Provinces meant that there was no great difficulty in pursuing part of the prescribed studies in a foreign country. For example, before the second world war we had a number of German Jesuit scholastics studying at the old Heythrop. In view of their future work, whether in Japan (in the case of one German Province) or in India (in the case of another Province) it would be an advantage to them to spend some years in an English-speaking environment, and the existence of a common programme of studies and the use of a common language as a medium of teaching greatly facilitated the covering of a large part of the prescribed ordination studies in England. Though, however, the old system had its advantages, there are obvious objections to conceiving the study of philosophy as a matter of absorbing provided proofs of pre-stated 'theses' for examination purposes. Mental ingenuity may be promoted in this way, but not real personal philosophical reflection. As for theology, the Biblical approach was markedly deficient. It is not surprising that the old system came in time to undergo extensive modification or change. Further reference will be made later to such developments.

As for my own attitude to my theological studies, I had little taste for moral theology, canon law and the like. In regard to Scripture, the lecturers in my day were doubtless learned, but it can hardly be claimed that their matter and manner were such as to arouse an enthusiastic response on the part of their hearers. To be sure, the lecturers no less than the students were victims of a system, and the criticism passed on them was often rather unfair. Scriptural exegesis was a notoriously thorny subject to tackle in those days. The Biblical Commission in Rome was intent on maintaining what passed for 'orthodoxy,' and it was suspicious of new ideas and adventurous lines of thought. The safest way of proceeding for a lecturer on Scripture in any ecclesiastical institution was to keep to familiar beaten tracks and not stick his neck out in any direction.

I took a considerable interest in systematic or dogmatic theology. I felt, no doubt, that the treasures of belief which my conversion to Catholicism had opened up for me in the first instance were being systematically explored. The trouble was that as a very large syllabus had to be covered in lectures, there was relatively little opportunity to go deeply into any particular line of thought. Still, I managed to do a certain amount of reading on theological topics which attracted my attention, such as the development of doctrine.

St. Ignatius Loyola, the founder of the Jesuit order, insisted that during the period of studies in preparation for life as a Jesuit priest, scholastics should rein in their zealous eagerness to pursue apostolic activities and give their minds seriously to the matter in hand, namely study. Similarly, they were not to neglect their studies in favour of prolonged prayer. At the same time St. Ignatius certainly did not envisage scholastics abandoning the life of prayer in order to give themselves exclusively to intellectual pursuits. The life of prayer was to inspire and feed, so to speak, application to study, and study should widen and deepen the understanding of God and his ways. The aim of our studies was not primarily to produce professional theologians or philosophers but to form Jesuit priests who would be whole-hearted followers of and co-workers with Christ. We were often reminded of such spiritual ideals and given opportunities of reflecting on and deepening our understanding of them, especially, of course, during the eight-day annual retreats but also at other times. We approached ordination, therefore, as a fuller consecration of oneself to God and his service. The professionally oriented studies may have tended to have what might be described as a desiccating effect, but the approach of ordination helped to counteract this effect.

In 1937, at the end of my third year of theological studies, I was ordained a priest by Archbishop Williams of Birmingham, in the chapel of Heythrop College, along with some sixteen other Jesuit scholastics. My father had died a couple of years before at an advanced age. I was present during his last days, though I doubt whether he was really conscious and aware of what I said. And I accompanied my mother and brother to the funeral at Trull church, where the suffragan Bishop of Taunton, who had been a friend of my father, gave the blessing. Though, however, my father did not live to see my ordination, my mother and brother were present, likewise my maternal grandmother. So was Father Valluet, the French priest who had received me as a schoolboy into the Catholic Church. Bob Woodbridge, my friend of Oscott days, was also there.

The next morning I offered my 'first Mass,' as it was inaccurately described (inasmuch as the newly ordained concelebrates with the Bishop during the ordination Mass). I remember the fact that I experienced great devotion during my early Masses as a priest; but in the course of time liturgical functions tend to become something of a routine, and though one can certainly try to resist this tendency, it is difficult, if at all possible, to recapture the first freshness with which one carried out priestly functions. This, I fear, is inevitable. If it is not to be expected that a married couple, however devoted they may be to one another after many years of married life, should be able literally to recapture the romantic love of early days, no more is it to be expected that in advanced years a priest should be able to relive at will the feelings which he experienced when newly ordained.

After Mass and breakfast I drove down to Taunton with my mother and brother and stopped at home for the permitted five nights. I then returned to Heythrop for the rest of the vacation and for the fourth year of theological studies. During this final year, when I and my companions in the 'long course' were preparing for comprehensive examinations covering most of systematic theology and a certain amount of philosophy, we were much less troubled by lectures (not at all in the last months of the academic year), and it was possible to combine study with some more obviously priestly activities. Thus for a large part of the year I practically had charge of a local country parish, as the priest there was dying. This meant cycling some distance on an empty stomach to say Mass, but I was only too glad to have the opportunity of exercising some priestly functions. Further, a plentiful breakfast was provided after Mass by a small convent of nuns, and this fortified me for the cycle ride back to the College and for continuation of my studies.

It would be understandable if the reader concluded from what I have hitherto said that if not ordination itself, then at any rate completion of theological studies would signal the definite end of one's period of 'probation' in the Society of Jesus. But if the reader jumped to this conclusion, he or she would be wrong. What was described as the Third Year of Probation (the two years of noviceship having constituted the first and second years) still lay before me. I spent most of the relevant period in Germany, and I propose to say something about this experience in the next chapter.

Chapter 7

In Germany Before the War

DURING THE COURSE OF MY HEYTHROP STUDIES IT BECAME clear to me that a good knowledge of German would be required for my future work. In the latest programme of ecclesiastical studies issued by Rome, study of the historical development of philosophical thought had been upgraded, and if, as seemed probable, I was eventually appointed to lecture on this subject, I ought to be able to read the works of the German philosophers in their original language. Greek I was supposed to know and reading French texts I could cope with all right, but I had never studied German. Here, of course, the presence at Heythrop of German-speaking Jesuit scholastics was a great help. As soon as I had acquired a more or less elementary knowledge of German, I started speaking the language with this or that German-speaker. Thus in the summer months I often went out for the day on a Thursday (our non-lecture day) and had a picnic lunch in the countryside. Sometimes we talked German and sometimes English, catering for one another's interests, so to speak. In those days Jesuit scholastics were certainly not encouraged to travel; but I managed to obtain permission to go to Germany during the summer vacation of 1936. As I wished to be able to practice German as much as possible and avoid places where I might encounter a number of

English-speakers, I chose to go to the noviceship and Juniorate of the East German Province of the Society of Jesus at a village called Mittelsteine in Silesia, not far from the small town of Glatz on the Neisse. (Since the second world war the area has belonged to Poland, and the names have been changed).

There was some very attractive country round about, and I remember walks and expeditions with young German Jesuits which gave me great pleasure, even if early starts and the energy displayed by my companions sometimes reduced me to exhausted silence, as on a memorable expedition to the Heuscheuer, in the direction of the Riesengebirge. Anyway, my spoken German improved considerably. Neither then nor later did I ever speak the language really well, but at any rate I made a good deal of progress in the weeks that I spent at Mittelsteine. At Mittelsteine the Nazis were not very evident, and I do not remember much talk about them. It is worth mentioning, however, that at the time of my visit the Master of Novices was Father Otto Pies, who was later consigned to Dachau concentration camp, where he did all he could to assist his fellow priests who were incarcerated there. He survived the war, and I was to meet him again at Münster. He was a fine man, and I greatly respected him. As for his young charges in 1936, I got on well with them, and I still retain pleasant memories of that Silesian summer.

At the end of the last chapter I referred to the Third Year of Probation, commonly known among Jesuits as the Tertianship. It was understandably assumed by the authorities of the Society that after long years of study, broken in most cases by periods of secular university studies or teaching schoolboys or both, the spiritual fervor of the noviceship would be somewhat diminished and that a more immediate spiritual formation for the priestly life was required. In the Tertianship therefore the priests who had recently completed their theological studies went through once again the thirty days retreat, though this time under the direction of the Instructor of Tertians and not the Master of Novices. They also studied the consti-

tutions of the Society and such like documents and gave
more time to prayer than was possible during the period
when they were supposed to be absorbed in philosophical
and theological studies. The Tertianship at that time
lasted ten months, though it was the custom for Tertians
to go out during Lent to take part in giving missions or
in some other priestly activity. When the Tertianship
was over, those who had been long enough in the order
could take their final vows. In my case, however, there
was no question of this, as I had not yet fulfilled the condition of having spent ten years in the Society exclusive
of ecclesiastical studies. Though therefore I made the
Tertianship on the completion of my theological studies, I
had to wait a good many years (seven to be precise) before I was qualified to take my final vows as a Jesuit.

The Tertianship of the English Jesuit Province was
St. Beuno's College near St. Asaph in N. Wales. Until
the foundation of Heythrop College in Oxfordshire it had
been the theologate of the English Province, and it was
there that the poet Gerard Manley Hopkins pursued his
theological studies. The house was beautifully situated,
with a fine view over the Clywdd valley to the hills and
mountains beyond. But it was not where I made the Tertianship. As I wanted to improve my knowledge of the
German language, I asked to be sent to a similar establishment in Germany or Austria, and arrangements
were made for another English Jesuit, Father Geoffrey
Sparrowe, and myself to go to Haus Sentmaring at
Münster in Westphalia. Apart from our Lenten activities
in England, our stay at Münster lasted from mid-Septem-
ber 1938 until mid-July 1939. Thus we started the Tertianship during the Czech crisis and ended it on the eve
of the second world war.

Having been told that we could go to Austria, if we
wished, to brush up our German before embarking on the
Tertianship at Münster, Geoffrey Sparrowe and I made a
leisurely progress to St. Andra in Carinthia, where we
stayed for some three weeks in the Jesuit noviceship. I
retain grateful memories of the hospitality and friendliness of the Dutch Jesuits at Rotterdam and the Hague,

who plied us with schnapps and cigars. At Frankfurt we were a bit lost in the large Jesuit College, but we were befriended by Father Kologrivov, a Russian who had been, if I remember correctly, an officer in the Imperial cavalry. He entertained Geoffrey and myself in his room and was a lively and charming host. He was the first Russian I had ever met. Moving on to Nuremberg, we found that unsavory Gauleiter Julius Streicher was due to make a public speech, and curiosity led us to make up our minds to be present at this open-air event. Unfortunately (or otherwise) we mentioned our intention at lunch to the Jesuit Fathers in the local Jesuit residence, and we were firmly told that it would be highly unfitting for two priests to listen to Streicher. Perhaps it was just as well that we did not go to hear the man. His newspaper was full of diatribes against the Jews, and also against the Catholic Church, and we gathered that the speech which we missed was hardly characterized by good taste, to put it mildly. In spite of offered explanations I have always found it a bit puzzling that people of the calibre of Streicher and his colleagues could come to the top and be listened to enthusiastically by a great many people in a country which prided itself on its cultural heritage.

When we set about leaving Vienna for Carinthia, the train was held up for three hours at the station. The chatty guard told us that this was due to troop movements, not a very encouraging piece of news. Anyway, the guard, who did not seem to be a man much afflicted by shyness, asked for a glass of the schnapps which Geoffrey and I had with us on board and said that he would return later for a Dutch cigar, as indeed he did.

In the circumstances it was late at night when we finally arrived at Klagenfurt, and we had difficulty in finding the Jesuit residence. We discovered the right square, but nobody seemed to know where the Jesuits lived. Or, if they did, they were not telling us. Geoffrey tried a house on one side of the square and came back with a red face and an embarrassed air, having unintentionally intruded on a lady about to retire for the night. Meanwhile I had found the Jesuit house and succeeded in rousing a lay porter, who had clearly been drinking copiously. His way of coping with the situation was to throw stones up at the Superior's window, until the poor man put his head out, to be told that two Englishmen were seeking admittance. In point of fact the Superior knew that we were due to arrive, but with the fall of night he naturally concluded that we had changed our plans. However, all was well. At Brussels I once had a similar experience, but the window, once opened, was then firmly shut again, and I had to go to a hotel for the night. At Klagenfurt things were done differently. The Superior, awoken, came down, welcomed us in the most friendly manner and insisted on giving us both a meal after our tiring and protracted journey. The next day, after an excellent lunch with the hospitable community, we went to St. Andra and settled in.

At St. Andra Geoffrey and I were each allotted a novice who came on most days to coach us in German. But there were plenty of other opportunities of conversing in German. For example, there was an elderly retired diocesan priest living in the house, who in his earlier days had been a Jesuit scholastic. A benevolent old gentleman, he loved talking, and after lunch, when we had drunk our *ersatz* coffee with the other Fathers, he used to invite Geoffrey and myself to his room for a cup of real coffee and a chat. I well remember an expedition we made with the good old fellow to a pilgrimage church, about twenty minutes distance away by bus. To fortify us for the hardships of the journey Dr. Hotzy (I may have misspelled the name) produced a paper bag at the start of the journey and presented us each with a slab of chocolate. When we had alighted from the bus, he insisted that a second breakfast was needed before we walked up the modest hill to the church. After descending the hill, it was, of course, time for a hearty lunch. Sitting about in the sun we saw a number of 'unreformed monks.' In the course of time life in the local monastery had become somewhat easy-going and, doubtless under pressure from Rome, a reform had been undertaken, but the monks who did not wish to accept the reform, were humanely permit-

ted to carry on as before until death, whereas new recruits would obviously be trained as reformed monks.
Hence the sight of some old monks sitting about in the
sunshine and surveying village life, while their reformed
colleagues were occupied in some more monastic pursuit.

There were several other interesting characters at
St. Andra. One of the Jesuits residing in the noviceship
was Father John Lenz, whose outspoken references in
sermons to the Nazis and their ideas and doings led to
his arrest towards the end of 1938. He was at first im-
prisoned in Vienna, and it looked as though the Nazi authorities had execution in mind. But in 1940 he was sent
to Dachau, whence he was transferred to Gusen, an off-
shoot of the terrible camp at Mauthausen. Sent back
after a time to Dachau, he remained there until the
Americans liberated the surviving inmates of the concentration camp. Later he published a moving book about
this experience, *Christ in Dachau.* By some standards
Father Lenz had obviously been unnecessarily imprudent,
making public statements which could hardly fail to result in his arrest. But he sincerely believed that, as a
priest, he had a duty to speak out plainly against Nazism
and its leading representatives. And in the course of the
centuries there had been plenty of precedents for his
attitude.

Also resident at St. Andra was a Jugoslav Jesuit
who had made some statement in a sermon to the effect
that the officers of the Royal Jugoslav army all suffered
from venereal disease. Why he should feel impelled to
make such an assertion, which, even if true, would be
hard to substantiate, is more than I can understand.
Anyway, he had consequently been accused of calumniat-
ing the Jugoslav army and had been sentenced to two
years in gaol. He succeeded, however, in getting into
Austria, and he apparently wanted to go to South America or some other foreign locality to work. Report had it
that the Jesuit General of the time said that the good
man would be much more useful if he went back to his
own country, served his sentence and then worked in
Jugoslavia. What happened eventually I do not know,

though I seem to recollect hearing that he left the Jesuit Order. If so, I imagine that this may very well have been what the Jesuit General hoped would happen.

The country round St. Andra was very attractive, and we made a number of excursions. On one occasion a small group of us had been up a neighboring mountain, a long and steep climb but in no way dangerous. Very sensibly we were all wearing open shirts. But when we got back towards the village, the Austrian Father who was acting as our leader insisted that we must wait until it was dark, as the villagers might be scandalized at seeing Jesuits so attired. I thought this absurd and said so. But all to no avail. We had to hang about until we could return through the village street under cover of darkness. It is difficult to imagine such an incident recurring nowadays.

When Geoffrey Sparrowe and I had spent three weeks at St. Andra, we thought that we at any rate spoke German sufficiently well to avoid being excluded from the Tertianship at Münster on the ground that we would be unable to understand and profit from the conferences delivered by Father Walter Sierp, the Instructor. But we were not due to arrive immediately at Münster, and we set off for Prague. The train was extremely late, and when we finally arrived at the Jesuit College we were taken at once to our rooms, without mention of any snack. However, we were both so tired by then that we did not mind and went straight to bed, being sufficiently fresh in the morning to tour what is one of the most beautiful of European cities. I had been there already, in 1936, but it was a delight to see once again the splendid Baroque churches, the famous Karlsbrucke, the castle and the cathedral of St. Vitus. In a shop I foolishly started talking German, whereas the lady behind the counter replied in French. Obviously, the proper thing to do was to start in English. Then if English were not understood, one could proceed in German. But if one were believed to be German, one was not exactly popular. Understandable at the time.

From Prague we went to Dresden, another city which I had included in my 1936 travels. Here poor Geoffrey was struck down by a bad attack of influenza and retired to bed in the Jesuit retreat-house. As it was clear that he would not be able to arrive at Münster on the appointed day, we decided that at any rate one of the two Englishmen had better arrive punctually and explain what had happened to the other. As Geoffrey was being well cared for, there was not much point in my staying on at Dresden and perhaps having to take to bed in my turn. To be honest, however, I did not want to miss a couple of nights in Berlin, though I felt rather guilty when Geoffrey told me later on that while he was lying in bed with a high temperature the Father Minister of the house, on his visit to the invalid, had offered consolation by saying that war might break out at any moment. As the Czech crisis was in progress, the Minister certainly had a point, but the possibility of war was hardly a helpful subject of conversation with an invalid who might become alarmed at the prospect of being interned.

At Berlin I unexpectedly came across a fellow English Jesuit, who had been doing some academic research in the city. As the political situation had made him very apprehensive, he asked me to accompany him to the British embassy to ask for advice about staying or not staying in Germany. As it was my job to arrive at Münster, I did not feel that his problem really concerned me; but I replied that I would willingly accompany him to the embassy, provided that he would first accompany me to the Unter den Linden for some real coffee and cream cake. After this fortifying visit to a cafe, where I noticed some very smartly turned out young German officers putting down rich cream cakes with an enthusiasm equal to that of any German housewife, we called at the embassy and naively asked for the ambassador, Sir Neville Henderson. An elegant young man, bearing the stamp of Winchester and New College, explained that the ambassador was, as we would appreciate, extremely busy. Would he, the elegant young man, do instead? Yes, indeed. The young man then remarked that though the embassy was not in a position to say whether war would break out or not, he would advise any British citizen to leave the country, unless he or she had a good reason for remaining and risking possible difficulties. My companion made up his mind to get out. We travelled together to the parting of the ways, where I turned off for Münster, while he went on to Holland and so back to England.

Most of my fellow Tertians were, of course, Germans. The foreigners consisted of Geoffrey Sparrowe, three Dutchmen and myself. If, that is to say, one does not count a Sudeten German as a foreigner. We foreigners naturally had to register with the police and pay a small sum. But when the Sudeten German went to the police, they refused to take any money from him. For in all probability, they said, he would soon be a German citizen through the incorporation of his part of Czechoslovakia in the German Reich. If this had not taken place by Christmas, he could return and pay for his residence permit. As things worked out, he never had to pay the fee, Germany having annexed the region from which he came. He was a quiet but, I think, rather romantic individual, and I had the impression that he felt quite proud at becoming a German citizen. What he thought about matters later, I do not know.

However this may be, I do not recollect any instance of unfriendliness being shown to a foreigner by any German Tertian for nationalistic reasons. I do not remember any cause at all for complaint on this account. The relatively young Germans were obviously in an unsettled state of mind, and some of the old and retired Fathers living in the house evidently considered the German Tertians as belonging to a rather inferior generation, which did not know how to behave with due decorum and gravity. Though, however, I could understand the old stalwarts' attitude, I tended to sympathize with their younger compatriots. They doubtless loved their country, and some of them at any rate found it difficult not to feel pride in the expansion of the German Reich and the recovery of the nation's power and self-respect. But they saw it dominated by a, in prominent respects, detestable regime, clearly headed for developments which might bring Germany either to a leading position in Europe or to utter destruction. Further, if the first of these possibilities was realized, the Church would be in for a very hard time. So it does not seem to be surprising if tension between a kind of sneaking pride in the achievements of the regime on the one hand and religious convictions and loyalties on the other tended to make the younger Germans restless, excitable and impatient of traditional ways and habits of mind. By contrast the Dutchmen were very solid and balanced persons. Anyway, the point which I wish to make is that the excitable state of mind of some of the German Tertians did not result in any hostility towards us foreigners.

The Tertianship was supposed to be a period of spiritual recollection, of prayer and of a renewal and deepening of the true spirit of the Society of Jesus as expressed by St. Ignatius of Loyola in his Spiritual Exercises and in the Constitutions of the Order. But in the actual circumstances, needless to say, peace and quiet and spiritual recollection were somewhat difficult to attain and retain. First there was the Czech crisis, the probable outcome of which sometimes seemed to be immediate war and which, for realists, did not appear to augur peace in our time. Then, on the 8th of November, 1938, there was an allegedly 'spontaneous' uprising of the German people against the Jews. In actual fact, of course, it was SS hooligans and toughs who smashed the windows of shops owned by Jews, dynamited synagogues and beat up Jews in the small hours in cities throughout Germany. It was a planned action, and it is difficult to suppose that the Nazi authorities seriously believed that the world would readily accept the claim that ordinary citizens throughout the Reich had risen spontaneously at two in the morning, armed with dynamite and possessing the technical skill to make the synagogues collapse on themselves, so to speak, without blocking streets with rubble.

On the following morning I had gone for a country walk with one of the Dutchmen, Father Piet Smulders, who later became a professor of theology in Holland.

Having lost our way, we approached a farm to ask for directions. The farmer saw us coming and seemed to be showing evident signs of terror. When we came near, he showed relief and told us the way. At the time neither Father Smulders nor myself knew what had happened the previous night. But when we heard the news at lunchtime, we understood the farmer's reactions. Presumably he was a Jew, and when he saw in the distance two black-clad figures coming towards him, he probably mistook them for members of the SS. When he realized that it was simply a case of a couple of priests, he was greatly relieved.

In the afternoon I went into the city with a German Tertian to survey the damage. Outside the destroyed synagogue there were a good many silent spectators, also some members of the SS, who seemed proud of their handiwork. My companion begged me not to make any critical comments. After all, the worst that could happen to me would be expulsion from the country, but he could be sent to a concentration camp. Naturally, I remained silent. Just as well perhaps, for I noticed that a shifty-looking little man crossed the road and stationed himself behind us, doubtless intent on hearing whether the priests said anything which he could report to the SS or Gestapo. Several worthy citizens were arrested that day in Münster for making critical or sarcastic remarks, though, for all I know, they may have been subsequently released after an unpleasant interrogation.

A few days later I happened to be in the city when a long funeral procession wound through the streets. There were long files of Nazis with torches, but no Christian emblems. I asked a gentleman standing nearby whose funeral it was. He looked apprehensive and then whispered that it was the funeral of a Nazi hero. After having given 'the German glance or look' (*der deutsche Blick*), that is to say having looked to see who was within hearing distance, he plucked up the courage to tell me that the funeral was that of an SS man on whom a heavy pane of glass had fallen while he was engaged in devastating a Jewish house or shop and who had later died in hospital. The Nazi authorities considered him a martyr to the cause.

In the local barracks there was a Jesuit laybrother, who had been called up for military service. About once a week he came to Haus Sentmaring for a meal, and shortly after the November 8th affair he told us how indignant his comrades were when they learned that the excellent Jewish doctor who looked after some of them had been pulled out of his bed by Nazi toughs in the middle of the night and so mishandled that (if I remember correctly) one of his legs had been broken.

There was a report that the Nazis intended to follow up their attack on Jewish synagogues and property with similar action against the religious houses, especially those of the Jesuits, and the Jesuit General directed that arrangements should be made with pious Catholic families to receive the German Tertians, if they were evicted in the middle of the night. Foreigners, such as Geoffrey Sparrowe and myself, were unlikely to be molested, intentionally at any rate, and could go to hotels if necessary. It appears, however, that the world outcry over the events of November 8th led the authorities to postpone their contemplated attack on the religious orders and their houses.

This did not, of course, prevent verbal attack. One day during our stay at Münster the Nazi Old Guard, the original followers of Adolf Hitler, arrived in coaches on one of their periodic tours, with Robert Ley sitting in the front coach. The city of Münster obviously had to entertain the visitors, whether it wished to do so or not, and after the evening banquet the Nazi heroes, well sozzled, roamed the streets calling loudly for the priests of Catholic Münster to be strung up to the lampposts. They did not, however, go beyond threats.

The city was also favored by a visit from Alfred Rosenberg, later to be hanged at Nuremberg. His previous attempt to get himself made a freeman or honorary citizen or what not had been thwarted by the redoubtable Bishop von Galen, but this time Rosenberg had succeeded in imposing his will. In the evening the eminent visitor made a speech in the town hall. We had to bear in mind the possibility that he might incite his Nazi hearers to descend on the religious houses in the city in the same sort of way in which they had descended on Jewish shops and places of worship. One of the German Tertians was acquainted with an SS man who still retained some religious belief, and his acquaintance had promised to try and get a warning through, if Rosenberg seemed to be whipping up his hearers to action. So the German Tertian remained in the road until the small hours, in case anyone arrived with a warning. But though Rosenberg spoke at length against the Church, he did not call for any immediate attack on religious houses, not even on the Jesuits. As I have suggested, the widespread outcry over the so-called *Kristallnacht* in November probably deterred the authorities from similar action for the time being.

When the German Jesuit Provincial paid his annual official visit to Haus Sentmaring, he asked me to tell the English Provincial, when I went back to England for Lent, that he could not guarantee the safety of Geoffrey Sparrowe and myself. If the house were to be invaded by Nazis, intent on violence and destruction, they might not take the trouble to discriminate between Germans and foreigners. I duly passed on this message to Father J. Bolland, who was English Provincial at the time, but he did not seem to be much impressed. During Lent I took part in giving two parochial missions, one at Gateshead, the other at Walthamstow. At the end of Lent, as there were strong rumours of an imminent invasion of Poland by Germany, I rang up Father Bolland and asked him whether or not Geoffrey Sparrowe and I should return to Münster immediately after Easter, as planned. "Of course, of course," he replied, "whoever heard of Tertians leaving the Tertianship before the appointed day?" So we returned promptly, as directed, only to find that the Dutch Provincial had told his three subjects to remain in Holland for the time being. They eventually returned three weeks late, after the war scare had died down for the moment. When Geoffrey and I were back in England in the second half of July, the Provincial remarked to me "You can imagine how anxious I was about you two during this last year." I felt like saying that in this case he had been remarkably successful in concealing his anxiety from us. But this would have been rude, and doubtless unfair as well. So I just smiled.

The period of the Tertianship did not, of course, consist entirely of a succession of alarms and excitements. We carried on the prescribed regular routine of prayer, study and so on; we helped out sometimes in neighboring churches; and we performed a variety of chores about the house. It seemed to me that the German leaders were bent on pursuing a path which would lead inevitably to war sooner or later, but our Instructor, Father Walter Sierp, who was also Rector of the house, did his best to keep us all calm, with our minds set on heavenly things. Thus we all made a pilgrimage to the shrine of Our Lady at Telgte. Father Sierp was an elderly Westphalian of solid and old-fashioned piety. We all liked him, but he was not perhaps very well suited for coping with the younger generation of German Jesuits. He had a marked predilection for the Dutch, understandable enough in a Westphalian. But I had the impression, justified or not as the case may be, that under his placid exterior he was very apprehensive of the future. One day, fairly early in the Tertianship, I went to him and asked him whether, in the event of Germany invading Poland and the Instructor being absent at the time, Geoffrey Sparrowe and I had his authorization to make straight for the frontier. For there would be an interval before Great Britain declared war, and we would have a good chance of crossing the frontier in time and so avoiding internment for the duration. Father Sierp replied that I should not worry about possibilities which might never be realized. I pointed out that I was not concerned with making prophecies but had simply asked a plain practical question. However, I got no answer out of the good old man, whether positive or negative. At the same time I am pretty sure that the Instructor was much more alarmed than I was, and that he was trying, vicariously as it were, to allay his own fears.

Looking back, however, I am inclined to think that I gave insufficient consideration and weight to his belief that it was his duty, as far as possible, to make the Tertianship a real spiritual event in our lives and to combat the intrusion of 'worldly' distractions and anxieties. (Unless my memory of events fails me, Father Sierp died during the war and did not live to see the final collapse of the regime, to which, with his deeply Catholic faith and loyalties, he was, of course, strongly opposed, even though he was careful what he said).

One real pleasure of my stay at Münster in 1938-39 was the friendship of Peter Wust, professor of philosophy in the university, to whom I eventually paid a tribute in the final chapter of my collection of essays entitled *On the History of Philosophy* (1979). Wust was born in a small village in the Saarland, the son of a local sieve-maker. As a boy he was possessed by an insatiable longing for books, a longing which it was difficult to satisfy in the circumstances. However, the village priest gave him free education, and as a result young Wust was able to pass the entrance examination for the Gymnasium in Trier and studied there from 1900 until 1907, when he went first to Berlin and then to Strasburg for university studies. In 1915 he was back again in his old school at Trier, this time as a teacher. During his studies he had lost the naive faith of his intensely Catholic early upbringing, but by 1923 he had regained it. He was then teaching at Cologne, where he enjoyed the friendship of the philosopher Max Scheler. From an early age Wust had been interested in philosophical themes, particularly in what one might describe as the metaphysics of the spirit. He was in fact a kind of Catholic existentialist, though minus the label. He published several philosophical books, and in 1930 he was appointed to the chair of philosophy at Münster. Some people were indignant that the relevant minister in Berlin had given the chair to 'an outsider,' who had hitherto been teaching in schools.

Early in my stay at Münster I made an appointment to call on Peter Wust at his home, and I prepared some questions about modern German thought, which I could

put to the Herr Professor and which would serve as an
excuse for my intrusion. I need not have bothered. Wust
started talking almost immediately about the political situation and gave me his frank opinion about the Nazis
and their policies, both internal and external. After some
time he hesitated, and I saw a look of alarm cross his
face. The cause for his concern was naturally clear to
me. Was this foreigner reliable and discreet? Wust
pointed out to me that he was a married man with children and that he could be put to death for treason as a
result of saying the sort of things which he had been saying. I assured him that I quite understood the situation
and the need for discretion, and during the months which
I passed in Münster I frequently heard from his lips tren-
chant comments on the ideas and exploits of the men who
ruled the Third Reich. Wust had no use whatsoever for
Nazism and its representatives.

Wust lectured in the university at 8:00 a.m., and at
10:30 he walked to the village of Mecklenbeck where he
drank coffee and discussed philosophical problems or simply chatted with his friend Dr. Vorholt, the parish priest,
after which he walked back to his house and got on with
his work. On Thursdays we were normally free, and on a
number of occasions I accompanied Wust on his walk. In
one respect at any rate he resembled Kant. He left his
house at exactly 10:30, neither before nor after. If one
was a bit late, one had to catch him up on the road. He
seemed to know all the children from the farms that we
passed on the way, and they evidently took to him. In
the lecture-hall he spoke as a man with a message, but in
ordinary life he gave an impression of childlikeness. He
died on April 3rd, 1940, after suffering for some time
from cancer of the lip. His farewell message to his students was not about philosophy but about the need for
prayer and the need to bear witness to the truth, the
truth which he himself had not hesitated to assert in the
classrooms of the university, notwithstanding its incom-
patibility with the Nazi creed. I do not mean that Wust
publicly denounced the Nazis or their ideology. It would
have done little, if any, good if he had used his professo-

rial chair to speak in the way in which Bishop von Galen was prepared to speak in the pulpit. He would simply have been despatched to a concentration camp, and his family would have been reduced to destitution. It was probably far more useful to expound a philosophy which was in fact opposed to Nazi doctrines. This, it seems to me, was the best service which he could render to his students. To be sure, it was not without its dangers, but at any rate he could not be accused of expounding ideas which were philosophically irrelevant.

As July drew near, one of my German companions told me that Father Sierp was looking for someone to take over a light 'supply' in a convent during the summer months. 'You need only say Mass daily, hear some confessions and perhaps say a few words to the nuns on Sundays. Nothing much is demanded, and you could give time to studying German. How about it?' I replied that there was going to be a war, and that I had every intention of crossing the frontier on July 15th, the day on which the Tertianship was due to end. My colleague retorted that even if Germany invaded Poland, England would not be involved; there would simply be another Munich-style agreement. Having been in England during Lent and feeling sure that there would be no repetition of Munich, I stuck to my guns and left Germany on July 15th. In point of fact it was not simply a matter of my choice. For it was my duty to place myself at the disposal of the Jesuit authorities in England for the summer period. I might be needed for some job while awaiting a more permanent assignment.

Chapter 8

Lecturing and Writing in Oxfordshire and Rome

AFTER COMPLETION OF THE TERTIANSHIP I WAS SUPPOSED to go to Rome to pursue two years of doctorate studies in philosophy at the Pontifical Gregorian University. But the outbreak of war put paid to this project, and I did not go out to Rome until I went there as a professor in 1952. Meanwhile I started teaching at the old Heythrop College in Oxfordshire, where I had already spent a good many years in ecclesiastical studies and which was consequently familiar territory.

When asked what I did during the second world war, I tend to feel somewhat embarrassed. With the building-up of the armed forces the supply of chaplains had to be increased, and I wrote to the Provincial of the period to put myself at his disposal. He replied that unless it became necessary, he preferred that I should give my time to teaching the Jesuit scholastics at Heythrop. Obviously, once conscription had been introduced, able-bodied young men could not enter religious noviceships or seminaries. And some who were already studying in seminaries or had joined religious orders but were not yet priests left the seminary or what not and enrolled in one of the armed forces for the duration. At the same time the Brit-

ish government exempted from conscription not only ordained priests but also those who had received the ton-
sure and minor orders and were thus technically clerics.
This meant that there would probably still be young
members of religious orders to be trained for future work,
and some people had to do the teaching. With an eye,
therefore, on the future of the Province and the mainte-
nance of schools the Jesuit Provincial wished to keep
Heythrop College going, even if with depleted numbers.
In point of fact the Jesuit Province supplied a large number of chaplains for the army and the air force. Thus
Geoffrey Sparrowe, who had been with me at Munster in
the year preceding the outbreak of war, served as a chaplain in the Royal Air Force in North Africa and Italy. I,
however, spent the war years in the relatively inglorious
occupation of lecturing to young Jesuits in the Cotswolds.

At Heythrop both students and members of staff (except, of course, those who were too old) did a good deal of
work on local farms, especially at the times when the
farmers were in special need of extra hands. And those
of us who were priests spent our vacations filling gaps of
one kind or another, in parishes or religious institutions.
At the same time the programme of studies in the College
was maintained, though classes naturally became progressively smaller. Apart, however, from the danger from
bombs jettisoned by German planes returning home from
raids on Birmingham or Coventry (one such bomb killed a
few rabbits in the vicinity of the College), we had little
contact with warlike operations. Those of us who went
fairly often to London naturally experienced the V-1's and
V-2's and might be witnesses to a large-scale raid on occasion; but while we were actually in the Cotswolds, we
were remote from the war, though from the terrace in
front of the College we could see the ominous glow over
London during a raid. I might add that in 1940, when
invasion seemed a real possibility, we took it in turns to
patrol the extensive grounds of the College in the early
hours of the morning on the look-out for German para-
chutists. Two of us wandered about with a whistle to
give the alarm to a colleague stationed on the roof of the

College. He in turn would then pass word by phone to the Home Guard or appropriate military post. I remember thinking that any sensible parachutist would deal with his discoverer before any alarm could be given. Indeed, roadblocks and other local defences were so primitive that one could hardly imagine an invading army being successfully checked in its progress, certainly not one of the calibre of the German *Wehrmacht*. However, we had the consolation of feeling that we were doing something at any rate to further the war effort.

Much later on in the war we saw piles of ammunition and weapons of various kinds being parked along country roads in the neighborhood. Our own drive was lined with crates of TNT, and the road from the College to the hamlet of Heythrop was used for storing the parts of aerial torpedoes. When the time of the Allied invasion came, all these deposits vanished practically overnight. And from my window I could see part of the vast aerial armada passing over.

As for my academic work, I lectured on Greek and medieval philosophy to second-year students and on modern philosophy to students in their third year. From the students' point of view the course lasted for two years, while from my own point of view it was a one-year course, in the sense that I covered all parts each year. This extensive coverage of western philosophical thought provided me with the background for composing my *History of Philosophy*. My first book, on Nietzsche, appeared in 1942 and had the good fortune of being recommended by the *Times Literary Supplement* and of being, generally speaking, favourably reviewed. I now have considerable reservations about the book, as indicated in the second edition (1975), but it is naturally pleasing to an author if his first book is well received. Interest in Nietzsche led to interest in Schopenhauer, and my book *Arthur Schopenhauer* was the result. Meanwhile I had turned my attention to the production of a general history of western philosophy, and the first volume, *Greece and Rome,* appeared in 1946. At the time textbooks on the history of philosophy used in Catholic seminaries were, in my judgment, inadequate and too brief, and my original intention was to produce a rather fuller work in three volumes, one on ancient philosophy, the second on medieval thought, and the third on philosophy from Descartes onwards. The projected second volume became two, and by the time both volumes had appeared, I had dropped my idea of covering the material in three volumes. Eventually the work consisted of nine volumes in hardback. I would have liked my *Philosophy in Russia* (1986) to constitute a tenth volume, but the publishers preferred to treat it as a work on its own.

As indicated above, I originally had in mind the production of a work for use primarily in Catholic seminaries. But when I found that successive volumes were being used in universities, especially in the United States, I consciously started writing for a very much wider circle of readers than those whom I had initially had in mind. Moreover, my approach to the subject-matter underwent some change. In my introduction to the first volume I raised the banner of Thomism, asserting my belief that there is a 'perennial philosophy' and that this perennially valid philosophy can be identified with 'Thomism in a wide sense.' Very orthodox claims from the point of view of official Catholicism at the time. As some critics noted, however, I also manifested a marked attraction to Hegel's idea of philosophy developing in and through the succession of systems and movements. In other words, while I explicitly identified the perennial philosophy with Thomism 'in a wide sense' (a saving clause), I also conceived Thomism, the perennially true philosophy, not as a body of static doctrines but as developing in and through the historically successive systems. It was clearly my hope that I would be able to show that this was indeed the case. But it is obviously somewhat difficult to argue successfully that the thought of St. Thomas Aquinas develops in and through the sucessive movements and philosophies which have arisen in the course of centuries, if, that is to say, the term 'Thomism' is to retain any distinctive and definite meaning, sufficient to mark it off from non-Thomist thought. It is therefore not surprising if I soon came to concentrate on throwing light on the connections between different movements and systems and on giving objective accounts of the thought of the various philosophers selected for treatment. Needless to say, if encouragement to pursue the goal of objectivity was needed, my awareness of the requirements of my potential readership provided it in good measure. To be sure, the concept of objectivity in history or, more accurately, historiography, is attended by a number of problems, a matter on which I have touched in the second chapter of my book *On the History of Philosophy.* But I see no sufficient reason for claiming that we can simply dispense altogether with the relevant concept. Even if for various reasons we cannot attain complete historical objectivity, we none the less obviously need to be able to distinguish between more and less objective accounts, more or less tendentious or fictional treatments. It may be the case that when some critics have drawn attention to my preoccupation with the goal of objectivity, they have passed implicit criticism on the rather noncommittal attitude which I have shown in a number of the volumes of my *History.* If so, this is understandable. But I was engaged in producing what might be described as an overgrown textbook, and I tried to restrict the amount of space devoted to critical evaluation. I wished to leave plenty of room, so to speak, for readers to make up their own minds.

If I started, as indicated in the introduction to the first volume of the *History,* by setting out to prove something, a thesis, as time went on I became more and more interested in the historical development of philosophical thought in West and East as a cultural phenomenon, related in a variety of ways to other cultural phenomena. I have sometimes been asked 'which philosopher do you follow nowadays?' This question, however, implies an attitude which, for good or evil, I have long tended to disregard. I can, of course, try to explain why I am attracted to this or that thinker (Karl Jaspers, for example), but I have become too influenced by the idea of historical development and by interest in the changing cultural roles and affiliations of philosophy as a cultural phenomenon to feel prepared to single out any one system as expressing *the* truth, a truth which other systems may aim at attaining but which they all in varying degrees fail to reach. As for different ideas of the nature and functions of philosophy (a highly interesting topic, in my opinion), these all belong to the history of philosophy. In other words, they constitute distinct phases in the life of philosophical thought.

Occasionally I have been accused by a Thomist stalwart (it might perhaps be better to say 'Catholic traditionalist') of propounding relativism. This is doubtless understandable; but I would wish to make a distinction. It seems obvious to me that in the course of its life human philosophizing has both influenced and been influenced by a variety of non-philosophical or extra-philosophical factors. The ways in which such influences have manifested themselves offer a wide field for exploration, and if I had the ability and were not already too old, I would very much like to pursue such exploration. Though, however, I am certainly interested in the ascertainable historical relations between philosophy and various extra-philosophical factors, it by no means follows that I defend or have any inclination to defend a purely relativist view of truth. I am prepared to claim that the concept of necessarily true propositions can be exemplified, that it is not an empty or bogus concept. I have said something elsewhere about this line of thought, as, for example, in my books *Philosophers and Philosophies* (1976) and *Philosophies and Cultures* (1980). Whether the remarks there made are sufficient to allay the fears of my accusers is, of course, another question. It may well be the case that in the eyes of an accuser the important aspect of the situation is not that I accept in principle the concept of necessarily true propositions and am prepared to cite an example or two but that I do not seem prepared to regard as necessarily true propositions all those assertions which he or she regards as basic in a sound Catholic apologetics.

When lecturing in the United States, I found that there existed an impression that 'Copleston' was the name for some sort of syndicate. This impression was quite incorrect. In the case of some earlier volumes of my *History*, a self-sacrificing colleague at the old Heythrop College, Father Trevor Paine, very kindly read the proofs and undertook the wearisome task of compiling the index. When, however, he left Heythrop for work in Africa, I had to compile the indices myself. Apart from this valuable help from Father Paine, which he asked me not to mention in my prefaces, I had no assistance. Indeed, until Heythrop transferred to London I had no secretarial help, though I used to get the final manuscript versions of texts typed in Oxford. If anyone is curious to know how I managed to write so much, the answer is, I suppose, that I did little else but study, lecture and write. Being celibate and having for most of my life no administrative post, I was able to devote a large part of each day to literary work. The syndicate idea was a figment of the imagination.

In 1952 I started lecturing in Rome at the Gregorian University during the first semester of the academic year, that is from October until February. The authorities had applied for me to join the staff to lecture on the history of philosophy; but what I was actually appointed to do when I got there was to lecture on metaphysics in the postgraduate course in the faculty of philosophy. This was not altogether to my taste. Moreover, I was expected to lecture in Latin, as this served as a common language for students from a variety of countries. Even if I was giving a seminar on modern British philosophy and all the students who were enrolled could speak English, I was none the less supposed to talk Latin. Nowadays the situation has changed. While main courses can be given either in Latin or in Italian, professors can use their own language in seminars and optional courses, provided at any rate that it is one of the better known European languages. Indeed, even in Gregorian life notable changes were to take place. When I was still lecturing there, the clerical students, who formed the great bulk of the student body,

had abandoned their cassocks of various colours (lobster
red in the case of students resident in the German College) for sweaters and jeans. Further, young ladies were
beginning to enrol as students, and the students had established a cafe-bar on the premises. By the time I gave
up teaching at the Gregorian, conditions had become
much more relaxed and humane.

By and large the staff were a very hard-working lot
of men. Students used to claim that if they visited the
university on Christmas morning to give their best wishes
to this or that professor, they encountered a profound silence in the corridors, broken only by the sound of type-
writers busily working in professors' rooms. There was
some truth in this story. There was not a great deal of
social life within the university building itself, not at any
rate at the time that I was teaching in Rome. The staff
met at meals, and we chatted for a while over coffee after
dinner. But apart from occasional gatherings of national
groups (my American colleagues kindly invited me on frequent occasions to their periodic get-togethers over a
drink), most of the staff devoted the greater part of the
time to their academic pursuits. If one was hungry for
social life, one had to look elsewhere. For my own part, I
wanted to carry on with my writing, and I grudged time
for purely social celebrations. At the same time I greatly
enjoyed my visits to the English and Scots Colleges (and
to the Beda), and I retain warm memories of the hospitality and friendliness accorded to me. I was also sometimes invited to meals by members of the British Lega-
tion to the Holy See and by the representatives of the
British Council, both of which were enjoyable occasions.
But I made no effort to penetrate Roman society, though
during Lady Boynton's visits to Rome, I met a number of
her Italian friends or acquaintances. (I have said something about the Boynton saga in another chapter.)

It was a pleasure and privilege to have as a colleague at the Gregorian the celebrated theologian and
philosopher Bernard Lonergan. Until the state of his
health compelled him to return to his native country, he
was the most profound systematic theologian at the uni-

versity. Some students would doubtless claim that he was also the most obscure. But at any rate with Lonergan's arrival the Germans no longer enjoyed a monopoly of obscure profundity. I should add, however, that at the social gatherings which the Americans arranged from time to time, as I have already mentioned, Lonergan was always simple and humorous. He was a very human person, besides being an outstanding theologian.

Bernard Lonergan and I often met on the Spanish Steps. Each of us was accustomed to take a walk after his siesta, and we frequently took the same one, though the other way round. As Lonergan's siesta lasted longer than mine, the result was that our encounters were often when he was climbing up the Steps and I was going down. I remember how on one such occasion I tried to allay what I thought was a groundless anxiety on his part. Some people had been photographing an actress or fashion model on the Steps (a by no means rare occurrence), and Bernard was apprehensive that a photograph taken while he was passing up might have included him and might appear in some paper. I tried to reassure him that it was unlikely that a photo would be published with himself in it, and that even if this did occur, it would not matter in the least. He would certainly look as though he were deep in thought, as doubtless he was.

It may be thought that as over a considerable period I spent several months each year in Rome, I must have learned to speak fluent and good Italian. This was far from being the case. To be sure, I acquired sufficient knowledge of the language for practical purposes. As Italian was the common language of staff, used, for example, over after-dinner coffee, one could hardly avoid acquiring a certain measure of fluency. At the same time the Italian spoken by most of us bore little resemblance to what was spoken in the street outside. During one of my visits to Rome I was asked by some students of the national university of Rome to give them some introductory talks on Wittgenstein. I did my best to make myself understood in Italian. But when the students started to play back one of the recorded talks, I asked them to turn off the machine. I had heard quite enough of my efforts to explain Wittgenstein's thought in Italian.

My journeys to and from Rome often gave me the opportunity to stay for a few days with an Italian friend of mine, the eccentric animal-lover, to whom I refer in another chapter. Further, when the semester had come to a close in February, I often lectured for the British Council in various centres, in the relevant Council Institute when there still was one (reasons of economy had led to the closure of a number of them), otherwise under the auspices of the local Anglo-Italian Society. I always enjoyed these little tours, not only because they gave me the opportunity of seeing more of Italy but also because they brought me in touch with a variety of Italians whom I would be unlikely to come across at the Gregorian. When someone in England asked me whether I preferred Heythrop or Rome, a friend who was with me intervened to remark that the real state of affairs seemed to be that I much preferred the time in between my periods at Heythrop and Rome.

I have naturally been asked on occasion how standards for the doctorate in philosophy in Rome compared with those obtaining in, say, the University of London. It is difficult to give a precise answer, for as classes or grades were awarded to successful candidates at Rome, standards actually achieved naturally differed. Some successful candidates, especially, of course, those awarded the grade of *summa cum laude* (equivalent to first class) were really as good as one could find anywhere, whereas it may well be the case (and doubtless was the case) that some of those who had to be content with a low or modest grade or classification would not have obtained a doctorate in philosophy in the University of London for work done. It is safe to say, therefore, that to obtain a doctorate at the Gregorian was easier than it would be in an English university. But this does not mean that a Gregorian doctorate was without any value. A *magna cum laude* was not awarded lightly, and still less a *summa cum laude*.

To return to life at Heythrop College in Oxfordshire. The College had been established in 1926 by bringing together the students of theology, plus their lecturers, from St. Beuno's College in N. Wales and the students of philosophy, plus their teachers, from St. Mary's Hall at Stonyhurst, all students and staff at the time being members of the Society of Jesus. Heythrop remained in effect a Jesuit scholasticate until 1965, when by an agreement between the Holy See, the Roman Catholic Hierarchy of England and Wales and the Jesuit order it became a Pontifical Athenaeum. This meant that Heythrop was entitled to confer Pontifical degrees in philosophy and theology not simply, as heretofore, on Jesuit students but also on non-Jesuit students, male or female, clerical or lay, who pursued courses of study at Heythrop and passed the relevant examinations. Heythrop was the only College with this status in Great Britain. The Archbishop of Westminster, Cardinal Heenan at the time, was appointed Chancellor, while the English Jesuit Provincial was Vice-Chancellor. I was named Dean of the faculty of philosophy.

Obviously, the extent to which Heythrop College could be expected to develop in its new status was pretty limited. For one thing, there would be no room in the College itself for many additional students, and building operations would have to be undertaken if the number of students were to increase on any considerable scale. For another thing, one could hardly expect the advent of a lot of students seeking Pontifical degrees, especially when there was a marked tendency for Rome to increase the length of the preparatory studies. The Dean of the theological faculty and general Director of Studies in the College, Father Bruno Brinkman, was both ambitious and optimistic, but I must confess that I felt considerable doubts about the success of the enterprise. It is true that a couple of religious congregations, the Salvatorians and the Montfortians, built halls of residence in the Heythrop grounds and sent their students to the College for their academic training. Further, some other orders or congregations which had houses in the neighborhood also sent us students. Thus Claretians came from Radford, Servites from Begbroke and Passionists from Broadway. Some diocesan students and also some Benedictines lived in the College itself, together with the Jesuits. We also had a few students from other religious denominations. For example, an Anglican married layman, who was then resident in the vicinity, studied for and obtained the Baccalaureate in philosophy, and two Ethiopians, a priest and a deacon struggled manfully, but not very successfully, with philosophical studies, while a gifted Romanian priest (later a bishop and assistant to the Patriarch of Bucharest) started his research for a theological doctorate at Heythrop in Oxfordshire, finishing it at Heythrop in London. But though the student body certainly became more diversified, it was obviously unlikely that students would flock to the Cotswolds for ecclesiastical degrees. The Catholic bishops were not prepared to abandon their seminaries, at home and abroad, and send the more gifted students to Heythrop after building a hall of residence in the grounds. Further, when Heythrop became a Pontifical Athenaeum and opened its doors to non-Jesuit students, the time was already near for a movement into some form of affiliation with an existing British university.

It was not only the student body which became more diversified; this development affected also the staff. Further, visits from outside lecturers became more common. For example, one year the inaugural lecture at the beginning of the academic year was given by the philosopher Gilbert Ryle, while another year it was given by Professor T. Torrance from Edinburgh, under the auspices of the theological faculty. I remember a learned American Rabbi giving a talk, also a representative of the Pentecostalists. On another occasion I invited Mr. Maurice Cornforth, the Marxist philosopher, to address us. Some of the old traditionalists disapproved of a Communist being invited to lecture, but the students raised no objection. Incidentally, they showed a considerably better knowledge of Marxism than the lecturer seemed to expect. Bishop John A.T. Robinson, of *Honest to God* fame, also visited the College and gave a talk. In other words, a good deal of fresh air was admitted. To put the matter in another way, the College was open to Pope John's spirit of *aggiornamento* and to the widening of outlook expressed at the second Vatican Council.

As mentioned above, when Heythrop in Oxfordshire became a Pontifical Athenaeum, I was appointed Dean of the Faculty of philosophy. It was then clearly desirable that I should be able to give my services entirely to Heythrop, and Cardinal Heenan, as Chancellor of the Athenaeum, made an approach to the Jesuit General. The latter accepted the point and told the Gregorian that it must look out for a successor. At first the time which I spent at Rome was curtailed, but at the end of 1968 I pulled out altogether. Father Garth Hallett, an American Jesuit and Wittgenstein scholar, came to join the staff for a while instead.

About 1965, partly under pressure from Heythrop teachers of theology, a new programme of studies was proposed, discussed and eventually accepted. But the new plan had hardly been implemented and got under way before the question arose of transferring the College elsewhere and forming links with a university which was able and prepared to take us under its wing. It may seem strange that with a fine, though aging and somewhat crumbling, mansion in the Cotswolds, a good staff and an excellent library, we should have chosen to pick up our belongings and move elsewhere, especially when we had just built a new library block at considerable expense (completed in 1965 and opened by Cardinal Heenan) and several religious orders or congregations had thrown in their lot with us, in some cases even building halls of residence in the grounds for their students. To a good many people it understandably seemed very odd that the English Jesuits, having accepted the status of Pontifical Athenaeum for their centre of studies and having invited bishops and other religious authorities to send students to Heythrop, should almost immediately announce their intention of moving house, away from the countryside and into a university. But it soon became clear that the new

Pontifical Athenaeum, situated in splendid, if healthy, isolation in the Cotswolds, was unlikely to flourish, and in view of the growing tendency, showing itself, for example, in the United States, for Catholic theological colleges to seek affiliation with a university or to move into an ecumenical situation (or, when possible, both together) it is not really surprising that the idea of moving the staff and student body of Heythrop College elsewhere began to be seriously discussed. The idea initially met with some opposition from ecclesiastical authorities, especially, of course, from those who had participated actively in obtaining for Heythrop the status of Pontifical Athenaeum and who were inclined to think that the Jesuits were letting them down or proposing to do so. But arguments in favour of the move were strong and in the end they prevailed.

Various possibilities were explored. Thus some of us visited Oxford, Bristol and Manchester to talk with reponsible university officials. In the end, however, it became clear that the University of London offered the most promising and attractive possibility. If Heythrop College were to be accepted as a School of the University, it could maintain its identity and at the same time become part of a wider whole, collaborating with existing theological Schools. Further (an important consideration) whereas in certain other centres which were considered a costly building-programme would have been required, it happened that the Sisters of the Holy Child Jesus were about to close their post-graduate College of Education in Cavendish Square, and they offered to lease the premises to Heythrop, if we decided to move to London. Again, the orders or congregations which had sent their students to us at Heythrop in Oxfordshire possessed houses in or near London where their students could reside while pursuing their studies at the College. Obviously, the Jesuits would have to reimburse those religious orders which had built halls of residence in the grounds of the old Heythrop (sale of the old Heythrop made this possible), but the choice of London meant that we would not be leaving their students in the lurch. They could still pursue studies at Heythrop.

Any further discussion of the move into London, which took place in 1970, is best reserved for a later chapter. Meanwhile I turn my attention to describing or mentioning some further aspects of my life and activity during the years when I divided my time between England and Italy.

Chapter 9

Back in Germany

AFTER THE SECOND WORLD WAR IT WAS THOUGHT DESIR-
able to 're-educate' the Germans. The French, needless to
say, were careful to provide lecturers for their zone. A
German once remarked to me rather caustically, "After
all, what have they got to offer but culture?" The British
authorities were also active. At that time, during the Allied occupation that is to say, the Foreign Office arranged
for lecture-tours and summer schools in the British zone,
and on several occasions I was invited to lend a hand.
Perhaps the authorities found that I did what I had
agreed to do and did not decamp immediately after giving
a lecture or two, leaving fraternization with students to
look after itself and swanning round the zone at the
taxpayer's expense. Besides, as I was a Catholic priest,
the authorities could be pretty confident that I was not a
member of the Communist Party and would not use a
visit to occupied Germany as an opportunity for propagat-
ing Marxism among German students. I came across one
or two lecturers who were doing precisely this. In fact I
travelled with one in the military train from the Hook as
far as Oberhausen or some such place. I found him an
affable and cheery individual, and I enjoyed his company,
but I was not altogether surprised to learn in course of
time that he had been using good old Shakespeare as a

vehicle for promoting belief in Marxism among German students.

My first visit to occupied Germany was made in 1947. At that time, soon after the war, conditions were still pretty grim. There was a great deal of devastation in the bombed areas, and there was a great shortage of accommodation. Further, of course, there was a serious shortage of food. Rations were insufficient and often unattainable. The German currency being practically worthless, farmers tended to keep their produce to themselves. Many people died of ailments such as influenza, because of their undernourished condition, and because of the acute shortage of fuel.

In a good many people's eyes the Germans were simply getting what they deserved. If children did not have enough to eat and if those adults who had not supported the Nazis were involved in the general calamity, this could not be helped. After all, if the victorious British had to put up with strict rationing and shortages at home, it was mere sentimentality to demand better treatment for a vanquished people which, in the main, had been only too ready to rejoice when its armies had conquered other countries and brought misery to many parts of Europe. The Germans were simply reaping what they had sown, and those in the western zones could be thankful that they were not exposed to the vengeance of Russia.

Needless to say, the Germans themselves differed in their attitudes. On a visit to Bonn I was invited by a parish priest, after I had taken part in a religious service, to take a glass of wine with himself and some colleagues. They spoke at length of the misery prevalent in Germany, and in criticism of the Allies. The general attitude seemed to be "it was better under Hitler." At the same time, as I noted in a diary, they all looked well fed and healthy. Again, a Catholic military chaplain told me that a highly placed German prelate had expressed to him the hope that he (the chaplain) could not sleep at night for thinking of the plight of the refugees from the eastern territories. When the chaplain replied that the

Poles also had had a bad time, the prelate answered that the Poles had always been a grasping nation.

Not all the German clergy were like this, of course. One priest said to the same chaplain, "We have learned nothing—nothing at all. If a new Hitler arose, the people would follow him at once." Again, a German driver once entertained me with a harrowing account of his experiences as a prisoner of war in Russia. When I expressed sympathy with the German soldiers who had to stay on in England for some time after the end of the war, the driver remarked, "The Germans would have done precisely the same if they had won the war." I could hardly believe my ears on hearing this doubtless correct but unexpected observation. It was not, however, exceptional. A British university education officer told me that while travelling in a train he had heard a German girl talking about the sad fate of the refugees from Polish-occupied districts. She went on to say that if she had the chance, she would like to tear the Poles to bits. At this a German gentleman broke in to say that the girl should remember how the Germans had treated the Poles. If everyone adopted her attitude, he added, there would be no way out of the circle of hatred and revenge. Further, the young lady should bear in mind the fact that the Germans did not help one another as they should. If the refugees were left to sleep in the open air or to herd together in bunkers, situations which helped to breed crime, it was quite unjust to lay all the blame on the Poles.

I do not want to pursue discussion of war-guilt, solidarity in guilt, the proportions of good and bad Germans, and so on. But it may be worth remarking that though a number of Germans were persuaded that the Allies were deliberately pursuing a policy of starving their erstwhile foes, this belief was quite erroneous. The Allies doubtless made mistakes, but they certainly did not set out to starve the German people. It was striking to see the way in which, once the western Allies had at length made up their minds to act independently of the Soviet Union and reform the currency in a drastic manner, farm produce became available in the shops practically overnight. It may have taken the western Powers too long to act independently of their eastern 'partner,' but it was not a question of their suddenly abandoning a deliberate starvation policy. There was no such policy.

I must admit, however, that in the conditions which prevailed when I first returned to Germany after the war I suffered a certain amount of embarrassment. For example, to see children begging for food and then to be whisked off to an English club to be given a good meal or treated to real coffee and old-style German cream cakes could be somewhat unsettling. I am not suggesting that members of the occupying forces and administration and visiting lecturers should have been subjected to the conditions prevailing round about. If any such policy had been pursued, the Germans would have looked on their victors as complete fools or as utterly incompetent. I merely mean what I have said, namely that the visitor could suffer some embarrassment, at any rate if he or she were in Germany only for a short period and had not had time to become hardened to the situation.

Even without indulging in a succession of black market transactions some Germans, of course, managed to do reasonably well. In 1947 a certain German university professor invited me to his house for lunch, perhaps in return for my having shared my breakfast with him on a Rhine steamer expedition. Though one could not, at the time, invite Germans into one's hotel, one was permitted to accept invitations, provided at any rate that one took something with one. So I had a packet of sandwiches made up at a Salvation Army canteen. In normal circumstances to arrive at a lunch with a packet of sandwiches would be considered extremely eccentric. But the circumstances were, of course, abnormal. However, my host took the sandwiches from me with a smile and explained that as he had a place in the country besides his house in the university town, he and his wife did not do so badly. And in point of fact the lunch, though by no means luxurious, was a perfectly reasonable meal. Incidentally, some years later, when Germany had made its recovery, I had an opportunity of visiting my friend again and spending a very pleasant evening with him over a bottle of Rhine wine.

In that 1947 visit I lectured in various centres, such as Bonn, Dusseldorf, Duisburg and Hamburg. At a summer school held at Bad Godesberg I see from notes that I gave a lecture on existentialism, which, according to my account, was liked by the students but found too clear and simple. This was, of course, a typical reaction. When lecturing in Germany, one ought always to include some unintelligible passages, if one hopes to escape the charge of having treated one's subject superficially and without depth. I remember asking a German, well before the war, for an explanation of some oracular utterances which he had made. When he gave me a lucid explanation, I asked why he had not expressed himself as clearly in the first instance. He replied with disarming frankness, "It sounds much more profound when expressed obscurely."

Most of the invited lecturers were perfectly competent, but there was one poor man who went off his head. He had already shown distinct signs of eccentricity, but one day he told the astonished students that he and his wife had created the world. When taken out to calm down, he started to eat burning cigarettes and rolled on the floor. Needless to say, he had to be taken to hospital. In the car he talked incessantly, I was told, and said, among other things, that I was the reincarnation of Pope Alexander VI, a broad-minded man who would stick at nothing. A somewhat dubious compliment. Anyway, I hope that the poor fellow made a complete recovery. The official responsible for inviting him to visit Germany may have felt a little embarrassed, when he or she heard what had happened.

In 1948 I paid three visits to Germany, the first to the American zone, the second to perform in a summer school near Cologne in the British zone, and the third to Berlin, during the blockade. I shall not easily forget the first of these visits. As far as I could make out, Washington had cottoned on to the fact that whereas the British and French had been doing a good deal in the cultural

line, the American efforts in this field were hardly conspicuous. It was therefore decided that money must be
allocated for sending lecturers round the American zone.
The occupation authorities accordingly got the names of a
host of possible lecturers through various organizations
and invited them to do their stuff. I had the distinct impression that the only real interest of the authorities in
the American zone was to be able to inform Washington
that a certain number of lecturers had been invited, sent
round the universities in the zone, paid off and returned
to their places of origin. I travelled out with another
British lecturer, and on our arrival in Munich we found
that no arrangements had been made by the Americans
for the lectures which we were expected to give, not even
for those which we were supposed to give that very afternoon in the University of Munich. In the end the authorities got on the buzzer to the university, and as a result I
was able to give a talk to about twenty people about recent British philosophy. My British companion was less
fortunate. Having arrived at a designated classroom and
being prepared to start his lecture, he was defeated by
the arrival of a German professor who, after taking a
vote among the audience as to their preference (the German won by a single vote), ascended the rostrum and
began talking. The Englishman had then to retire as
gracefully as he could. As for other centres, such as
Regensburg, Erlangen and Wurzburg, a German representative of the Bavarian ministry of education kindly tele-
phoned to the various universities and told them to expect us when they saw us. In the event the relevant professors were very good about handing over their audiences to the visiting lecturers when they turned up.

The Americans provided the other Englishman and
myself with a car and driver and asked whether we
would take along a Swiss Member of Parliament who was
also on the lecture-round. We were somewhat surprised
to find the Swiss giving directions to the driver and be-
having as though he were taking us along, rather than
the other way round. But we soon realized that the
Americans must have told the Swiss that they were allot-

ting him a car and a driver and asked whether he would
be so kind as to take along a couple of British lecturers.
Anyway, the three of us got along all right together.
When we finally arrived at Frankfurt, the military government representatives did not ask us a single question
about the cultural side of our tour, though they presented
us with generous cheques. I imagine that they must have
heaved a sigh of relief when the horde of lecturers was at
last off their hands and they could report to Washington
that the sum of money set aside for the promotion of culture had been duly spent.

As for the Berlin visit, I must have prepared pretty
carefully for it, as I find in a notebook a list of a hundred
and twenty-one questions to which I wanted answers.
They are grouped under the headings of university life,
schools, the Technical University, youth organizations, social affairs, the Catholic Church in Berlin and the Russian Zone, relations between the Catholic and Evangelical
Churches, the work of the Society of Jesus, and miscella-
neous. Most of the questions, I see, received brief answers. They were put to British officials, to professors
and students of the Humboldt University and of the Technical University, to the Cardinal of Berlin, to various
priests and pastors, to German Jesuits, to taximen and to
anyone who seemed to be able to offer information.

At the time the famous Berlin wall did not yet exist,
and one could go more or less where one liked, provided
that one did not make any attempt to leave the city itself
and enter the Soviet Zone without a permit. As for the
Russian sector of the city, I entered it on several occasions and was never asked to show my passport. I must
admit, however, that the British authorities were not at
all keen on such excursions, and they liked to be informed beforehand when and where one was going. After
all, if one got involved in any incident, it was they who
would have the trouble of dealing with the matter. Anyway, I kept to the main streets and did not attempt to
enter into conversation with strangers. When in the Russian sector, I visited the 'House of Culture,' where there
was an exhibition of Soviet art from Moscow. I cannot

say that I was favorably impressed, and I do not suppose that German viewers were favorably impressed either.

The lectures on philosophy which I gave to mixed audiences of students and general public were delivered at the British Information Centre in the Kurfürstendamm. At a lecture on existentialism a professor from the Humboldt University in the Russian sector had been invited to take the chair. Someone had warned me beforehand that I must be prepared for being called a reactionary or even a Fascist, but the professor, who had suffered a good deal under the Nazis, was perfectly polite and friendly. He did indeed indicate that in spite of my criticism of certain aspects of existentialism, I was still too sympathetic to it for his liking. But this was said with a courtesy and tact which were rather lacking in the utterances of a professor from the Technical University in the British zone, who took part in the discussion following the lecture.

At a lecture which I gave on British philosophy the chair was taken by another professor from the Humboldt University, this time a lady. On another day I had a meeting of about three hours with her and a few of her students. She told me that questions had been asked by Russian supervisors of the university about her lecturing on philosophers such as Leibniz and Kierkegaard. As for Hegel, why, it was asked, did she treat of his philosophy of history and of religion? Hegel's ideas on these topics were, she was told, reactionary; she ought to devote her attention to his logic. When she urged that from the pedagogical point of view it was preferable to start with more easily intelligible material, she was informed that in Russia Hegel's logic constituted bedside reading with farm laborers. She told me that, as she was not considered altogether ideologically sound, she found herself receiving smaller and more infrequent food supplements from the Russian authorities, whereas professors who were deemed more acceptable received a big package weekly.

Though the good lady was managing to get along, she felt that a change was desirable. I am not sure what happened in the end, but my impression is that she moved to the so-called 'Free University' when it was set up in the American sector. At that time at any rate I do not think that there was any faculty of philosophy in the Technical University in the British sector.

At the Anglo-German club I had a long talk with a German who had been a professor of history at Berlin. He had written something of which the Russians disapproved, and one day a Russian officer invited him to make a visit in a car. Getting into the car, he was at once whisked off to prison in Saxony for nearly a year. Most of the time he had very little to eat, but after some eight or nine months the Russians started to feed him up. At the end of the process they not only released him but offered him a chair at Rostock. When he declined the offer, they let him return to Berlin. He told me that during his time in prison he had formed the impression that the ordinary Russian knew precious little about Christianity but had no pronounced anti-Christian feelings. Though he was a priest, he did not experience from his captors the sort of antipathy felt towards the clergy by members of the Nazi SS. Indeed, Russian officers sometimes asked him questions about religion. They refused, however, to believe that anyone could really lead a celibate life.

I made further lecture-tours in Germany in 1954, 1956 and 1957. By this time, of course, conditions in the Federal Republic were very different from those prevailing during my first post-war visit to Germany in 1947. Further, whereas in 1947 staff and students were still suffering from a prolonged lack of contact, on both the personal and literary levels, with staff and students of other western countries, in the fifties this situation had undergone a marked change, a change which could result in rather embarrassing situations. For example, when I was invited to undertake the 1957 tour, I offered Wittgenstein as one of the subjects on which I was prepared to lecture. This topic was chosen by the relevant department heads at Mainz and Münster. Assuming not only that I would be talking to general student audiences but also that the audiences would know little about

Wittgenstein, I prepared a lecture in which I outlined and compared some main lines of thought expressed in the *Tractatus* and the *Philosophical Investigations*. To my dismay, however, on arrival at Mainz I found that I was expected to read a paper to an audience consisting of lecturers, 'assistants' and members of the professor's philosophical seminar who had already studied Wittgenstein's writings. To be sure, the professor did his best to put me at my ease, but all the same I felt that my talk hardly came up to expectations, being far too elementary. At Munster the situation was in one respect even worse. For I discovered that the flourishing department of logic possessed copies of the then unpublished writings of Wittgenstein. In another respect, however, the situation was much easier than at Mainz. For the Münster lecture was open to students in general, so that a broad treatment of the theme was not inappropriate. As I was given a standing invitation to return, the results of my efforts may not have been as bad as I feared that they might be.

Though embarrassing for me, this sort of situation can hardly be described as most unusual. Lecturers are not infrequently left without sufficient previous knowledge of the kind of audience which they are to address and of what is expected of them. When a lecturer comes out of the blue, so to speak, he or she may easily underestimate the audience's background knowledge. Alternatively, he or she may give a lecture which passes over the heads of a large proportion of the hearers. When a lecturer is very famous, such as Bertrand Russell or, in theology, Karl Barth, this may not matter much, as probably a fair number of the audience simply want to see the lecturer, without bothering much about the content of the talk. But with lecturers of less exalted status some fairly precise previous briefing is highly desirable, whenever possible.

Let me add a couple of anecdotes relating to visits to Germany not long after the end of the war. The first incident occurred while I was walking in a street in Würzburg. I had come to a crossroads where traffic had got held up by red lights. Suddenly the driver of a lorry which had had to stop jumped down from his cab, hurried to the pavement, greeted me warmly and then darted back to his cab as the traffic started to move on. He was an ex-soldier who had been in a German prisoner of war camp near the old Heythrop College in Oxfordshire. I had looked after the religious needs of Catholic inmates during the last part of the war and for some time afterwards, and I had also obtained German books for the camp library and attended various modest festivities organized by the prisoners in general. I was both surprised and pleased that a former inmate of the camp had recognized me so quickly and put himself out to greet me.

The other incident, I think, took place rather later. On one of my visits to Munich I was asked by the representative of the British Council (which took over from the Foreign Office after the occupation) to give a talk, simple if possible, to students of a language-school. Before the talk I was taken to see the Director in his room. He certainly looked German, but his English was so good and so free from any non-English accent that I asked him what part of England he came from. He replied that he was German. When I apologized for my mistake and remarked that his English was extremely good, he commented "So it ought to be; after all, I was Adolf Hitler's interpreter." I felt rather a fool. I must have been informed that the Director was called Dr. Schmidt, but I do not recollect having been given any further particulars in advance about the bearer of this not uncommon name.

My visits to Germany in the years following the war were not confined to lecture-tours. One summer, when the Federal Republic was already well established, I spent several weeks at the little Jesuit residence in Stuttgart and helped out in activities of a religious nature during the serious illness of a friend of mine. Later on, in the early seventies, I took the place of a parish priest in the Eiffel region, while he had his holiday. But I doubt whether any reader would be really interested in such doings. So I will close this chapter by making some reflections prompted by my experiences in Germany during the period of occupation by the western Allies.

My contacts with members of the administration of the British zone were more or less confined to people concerned with education. Though I hardly came across them, I have no doubt that the high-ups were thoroughly competent persons, who had held and would again hold responsible positions in Britain by reason of the intrinsic merits of their services. As for their subordinates, however, it was certainly possible to find people occupying important positions, such as supervising secondary education over a large area of the zone or serving as an university education officer in this or that German university, who would be very unlikely to occupy comparable positions back in Britain. This was, of course, understandable. If, for example, someone either already had a good post in Britain, with a prospect of promotion, or if someone saw a real chance of obtaining such a post, he or she might well be reluctant to serve in the administration of occupied Germany, when it was clear that the duration of the occupation, and so of the relevant post, was uncertain and unlikely to be protracted. On return to Britain, the person might find it difficult to get the sort of job he or she wanted. At the same time service in the administrative set-up possessed obvious attraction, and it is not surprising if encounters with some officials made one wonder how they came to be enjoying a degree of responsibility and power which they would be most unlikely to have back in Britain. One might also feel prompted to wonder what the Germans really thought about the situation and about our claims to be re-educating them.

Let me try to prevent possible misunderstanding of what I have just been saying. It is doubtless true that all occupations, including the British occupation of part of conquered Germany, have provided a number of individuals with the opportunity for pursuing questionable activities. But wholesale denunciations of the Control Commission and its personnel were unjust and based on shaky generalizations. Further, even if in the occupied area an official has been entrusted with power and responsibility which he or she would be unlikely to enjoy back in the home country, it by no means follows that the person concerned is not endeavouring to carry out assigned duties in a conscientious and efficient manner. Of my personal contacts with British officials in the education branch, and also in the religious affairs branch, I have nothing but pleasant memories. They were, as far as I can recollect, uniformly helpful and friendly. They were efficient in their arrangements, and they did not make me feel that they were performing unpleasant chores, which had to be got through somehow or other. I felt a real respect for the men and women who exerted themselves to do their jobs conscientiously, and whose friendly attitude made the activities of a visiting lecturer much more agreeable than they might otherwise have been.

Looking back on my post-war visits to Germany, I feel certain that the international summer courses sponsored by the Foreign Office and the education branch in the British zone were well worth while. It was of real value to German students to have the opportunity of meeting and living with students from Great Britain and other countries. I do not mean to imply that the summer schools were of value only to Germans. They were also of value to non-Germans. As for the lecturers, though these were doubtless required for academic meetings of the kind which I have in mind, the really important aspect of the gatherings was, it seems to me, the promotion of good international relations and the growth of mutual understanding. It is greatly to the credit of the British authorities that they actively encouraged developments of this nature.

Chapter 10

Lecturing in Various Countries

THERE WAS A TIME WHEN A CERTAIN SECTION OF THE press was taking every opportunity of saying or implying something to the detriment of the British Council. The money of the taxpayer, it was said, was being spent on providing novels for benighted foreigners to waste their time on. Again, lecturers were swarming round Europe or even much further afield at the public expense. And so forth. Behind this campaign there lay a story and, it appeared, a personal grievance which expressed itself in appeals to ignorance and to philistine prejudice. Happily, the British Council continued to fulfill the very useful functions which, one hopes, it will go on fulfilling. The Council has done and is doing a great deal to represent British cultural life in many countries, to promote international relations on this level, and to develop cultural exchanges. For my part, I am proud to have had the privilege of some slight association with its work at various times.

Sometimes, of course, it was simply a question of giving lectures for the Council in one or two centres in the course of a tour undertaken under other auspices. This was the case in my first lecture-tour in Spain, many

years ago. Sometimes it has been a case of undertaking
lecture-tours for the Council when I was already in the
country concerned, as happened during the years when I
was teaching regularly at the Gregorian University in
Rome. Occasionally, however, I have been invited by the
Council to go out from England on a lecture-tour. A visit
to Austria and Switzerland in the second half of November 1959 falls into this third class.

In the last-mentioned tour I remember two somewhat embarrassing incidents. In Austria I rashly consented to take part in an unrehearsed radio interview,
and I imagine that the results were pretty disastrous
from the linguistic point of view. In Switzerland I allowed
myself to be provoked into making some regrettably undiplomatic remarks. This happened in Zürich. I had
given a lecture to the Swiss-British Society on Bertrand
Russell as a humanist, and after the lecture there was a
dinner. The president of the Society, a Swiss schoolmaster, devoted his after-dinner speech to a defence of the
passing of paragraph 51 of the Constitution which barred
the Jesuits and certain other orders from conducting religious and educational activities in the country. He was
not, of course, attacking me personally, but he did attack
the role played by the Jesuits at the time when the confederation came into being. It is true that the good man
added that the relevant law or paragraph should nowadays be repealed, but I thought it rather odd that he
should have chosen this particular topic for a post-prandial speech to celebrate my visit. As he had a typed
speech before him, the choice of theme can hardly have
been prompted by anything said in my lecture on
Russell's humanism. Anyway, I should, of course, have
made some humorous allusion to his remarks about the
Jesuits and left the matter there. As it was, however, I
am rather ashamed to recall that in my reply to the
president's speech I referred to the fact that Norway,
which had had a much more stringent anti-Jesuit law,
had recently repealed it, as inconsistent with the ideals
expressed in the Atlantic Charter. For good measure, I
added that Norway, an almost entirely Protestant coun-

try, had shown a generosity and tolerance which Switzerland, a country with a large number of Catholics, had hitherto failed to show. I admit that my remarks were somewhat unfair. For whereas the Norwegian parliament was able by itself to repeal the relevant law, in the case of Switzerland a referendum would be required, as a paragraph in the Constitution was involved. However, I had been nettled by what seemed to me at the time gratuitous criticism of the order to which I, a dinner-guest belonged, and my observations must have sounded as though I regarded Switzerland as narrow-minded and stuffy.

During these unfortunate proceedings I noticed that a number of people at the table were looking down their noses, whereas a diplomat from the British embassy in Berne seemed highly amused by these undiplomatic goings-on. I shudder to think of the comments he may have made when he got back to Berne.

It should be added that the idea of repealing the law had been mooted and discussed more than once. The difficulty was that the matter would have to be put to a referendum. The outcome would be uncertain, and in any case fanatics would be provided with an opportunity to make trouble. The authorities thought that the wisest policy for the time being was to leave the situation alone, while doing little or nothing about modest infringements of the law, provided that formal complaints were not made by interested parties. However, when a revised version of the Constitution came to be submitted for a referendum, the relevant paragraph was quietly dropped, and the package-deal, so to speak, was accepted by the people. This happened some years after the incident described above.

In late February and early March 1964 I lectured for the British Council in Spain and Portugal. After my lecture at the British Institute at Madrid I was asked by the headmistress of the English school to give a talk on the following morning to the older pupils of the school on the theme 'What is philosophy?' As the audience would consist of boys and girls about thirteen or fourteen years old, I did not relish the prospect. But I felt that it would be ungracious to refuse. So I tried, with or without success as the case may be, to make matters as simple as possible. At Lisbon I was faced with a similar situation, and I see from my notes about the tour that a good many questions were asked after the talk, mainly by 'the female part of the audience.' Besides giving a lecture in the British Institute at Lisbon, I also gave three lectures in the university. The talks to school children at Madrid and Lisbon were, of course, uncovenanted extras.

During my visit to Spain I naturally steered clear of political discussion. But I was interested to hear the opinions of some professors on such thorny topics as the influence of Opus Dei in academic life. In a certain city a university professor complained bitterly that posts could hardly be obtained in the University of Madrid, in some faculties at least, except through the patronage of members of Opus Dei. That is to say, the Opus Dei was in a position to block appointments. I do not know to what extent the professor's statements were accurate, but I heard similar remarks from others.

In universities and in centres such as Florence or Madrid one could, of course, talk on philosophical topics, provided that one chose a theme of sufficient general interest and tried to avoid technical or esoteric language as much as possible. Indeed, a philosopher would obviously be expected to talk about philosophical subjects. But in small centres or in addressing teachers of English and members of, say, an Anglo-Italian society, who were primarily interested in hearing something about England, I offered, besides some philosophical subjects if such were required, themes such as the Public Schools and the English university system. The lecture on the Public Schools, which not infrequently was chosen, was not intended to be propaganda on behalf of the Public School system. Nor was it designed as an attack. I tried to explain how the system arose and to illustrate some of the strong and weak points of the schools in question. My hearers' reactions differed considerably. For example, the idea of boarding-schools, coupled with the segregation of sexes (changes in this respect had not yet begun), tended to be repugnant to Italian convictions about the importance of family life. Sometimes, however, criticism was directed primarily at what was taken to be the undemocratic and anachronistic nature of the Public School system. While sympathizing with a good deal of the criticism, I pointed out the folly of abolishing independent schools simply on ideological grounds, when no really adequate alternative had been yet developed. Again, it was all very well to talk about unfair educational advantages. But it was not as though the State were involved in the expense of maintaining such schools. It was the parents who did the paying. And if the State developed adequate alternatives within its own system, one could reasonably expect parents to make increasing use of what the State provided. Anyway, however all this may be, topics such as the Public Schools could give rise to some fairly general and lively discussion.

To turn from southern to northern Europe. In 1959 I was invited by the Academicum Catholicum (corresponding more or less to the Newman Association in this country) to undertake a lecture-tour in Denmark, Sweden and Norway. I spent about a month altogether in Scandinavia, lecturing at Aarhus and Copenhagen in Denmark, at Lund, Stockholm, Uppsala and Göteborg in Sweden, and at Oslo in Norway. During my tour it was suggested that I should take in Finland too. But at the time I felt that I had had enough travelling. Later, of course, I rather regretted my decision.

Before my visit to Scandinavia some German friends had told me that I would be wasting my time if I discussed metaphysical problems. My best plan, in their view, would be to give factual and descriptive lectures about current British philosophy, even if this turned out to be a case of carrying coals to Newcastle. In Scandinavia, I was informed, there was a widespread indifference to religious belief, which went hand in hand with a lack of openness to metaphysical themes. As, however, the invitation had come from a Catholic organization and as everyone concerned knew perfectly well that I was a

Catholic priest, I did not think that it would be appropriate if I restricted myself to descriptions of British philosophy, especially as this would certainly be pretty well known already. I would obviously be expected to attack positivism, either directly or indirectly. And I made up my mind to do so. To be sure, in England logical positivism was already regarded as outmoded by the more fashionable philosophers, a fact which made me wonder whether I might not be found guilty of flogging a dead horse. I need not have worried. To be sure, I found that some professors who had been described to me as positivists were in fact more akin to the linguistic analysts than to members of the Vienna Circle. But a positivist mentality was sufficiently widespread in academic philosophical circles to render groundless my fears about the relevance of criticism. So at any rate it seemed to me.

In one university, which I visited at an early stage of my tour, the professor of philosophy, who honored me by his presence at my lecture, showed some signs of annoyance at what I had to say about positivism. This rather surprised me, for he knew that I proposed to adopt a critical attitude to positivist thought. But it may very well be that he had expected me to refute positivism by appealing to Thomism or even to Christian doctrines and was not well pleased when I represented it instead as an antiquated position, incompatible with advances made in the analytic movement, and as an intrinsically deficient theoretical justification of an attitude fostered by extra-philosophical factors in a given cultural situation.

On my visit to a Swedish university I came across a marked resistance to Wittgenstein's later ideas about language. It seemed, indeed, to be mainly motivated by the desire for a unitary standard or norm, provided by an ideal logical language, for assessing what *the* meaning of a proposition must be. But I thought that in some cases other motives were certainly present. One well known Swedish philosopher, Professor Hedenius, told me that he preferred Bertrand Russell to Wittgenstein, Austin and other such thinkers; and as Hedenius was noted as a resolute critic of Christian belief and ethics, it was not unreasonable to see in this preference an expression of his attitude on such matters. After all, it is not so easy to use the later ideas of Wittgenstein as weapons to attack Christian belief and moral convictions. And even though Austin was not himself a man of religious faith, we can hardly regard the mapping-out of ordinary language as constituting, in itself, a grave menace to Christian belief and ethical doctrine. As Hedenius saw, for anyone who wishes to conduct an anti-Christian campaign, Russell makes a better hero than Wittgenstein.

After a lecture which I gave at Oslo under the auspices of the British Council (I forget on which of my two visits to the Norwegian capital) and which the then British Ambassador honored by his presence, a Norwegian youth came up to me and startled me by saying that he was soon off to Caldey Island, off the Welsh coast, with the intention of living as a hermit. He was a Lutheran, I ascertained, and he seemed to be interested in mysticism. What happened to the youth I do not know, though I have often wondered. Anyway, though I found the Danes more attractive than either the Swedes or the Norwegians, it seemed to me that in Norway there was a greater degree of openness to a religious vision or interpretation of life.

In forming this impression I may have been over-hasty and mistaken, but a later visit to Oslo seemed to confirm it. On this visit I had been invited to participate in an international seminar on ethical problems, in which scientists, philosophers, psychologists and sociologists of very different outlooks took part. Towards the end of the seminar an open session was to be held in the university, at which Professor Hedenius from Uppsala and I were to confront one another on the subject of religion in the world today. The hall was crowded, and it seemed to me that the majority of the students were in sympathy with my line of thought (rather Teilhardian in approach) rather than with that of my colleague. I am not suggesting that I spoke better than Hedenius. I am suggesting that a good many Norwegian students were glad to hear a non-positivist interpretation of reality offered for their reflection.

I gathered that in lectures and broadcast talks Hedenius was accustomed to use Catholicism to attack Lutheranism. That is to say, he argued that from a rational point of view Catholicism was a more coherent and better grounded system than Lutheranism. The former, after all, tried to provide a rational basis for faith. Having established this point to his own satisfaction, Hedenius then went on to claim that a man of the twentieth century could not be expected to accept Catholic beliefs or Catholic moral teaching, especially, of course, traditional Catholic teaching in the domain of sexual ethics. Hedenius was a clever man and a good speaker, but his thought was predominantly critical, and I think that he came to leave a good many young people quite unsatisfied.

Incidentally, I found some signs in Lutheran theological circles of a real concern with the problem of the relation between reason and faith. This was understandable. If philosophy is treated as a kind of game played in academic preserves, and if philosophers disclaim any connection between their pursuits and religious belief or concrete moral judgements, theologians can more easily disregard philosophy as irrelevant. But if philosophical argument is used, as Hedenius used it, to criticize and undermine theological beliefs and moral convictions, some theologians at any rate are likely to find it an unsatisfactory policy to say simply that 'it is all a matter of faith.' Some at least are likely to look for a rational basis for faith, even if at the same time they are understandably alive to the danger of making religious belief logically dependent on any one particular philosophical system. Thus when I gave a lecture at Uppsala on the relation between reason and belief in God, some Lutheran clergy and students were present, and whatever they may have thought about the content of my talk, they certainly seemed to be interested in the topic. Later on I was invited to return to Uppsala to conduct a seminar on this sort of topic. Illness prevented my actually going back to Sweden for this purpose. But the fact I had been invited presumably indicated some interest.

As for the United States, in the sixties I made a number of lecture-tours, taking me from Boston and New York in the east to San Francisco in the west, from, say Dartmouth in New Hampshire in the north to New Orleans in the south. The institutions visited included secular universities, state and private, Catholic universities, and other academic establishments. But I have no intention of trying to reconstruct all my itineraries or to recount all my engagements. Of the tours as a whole it is sufficient to say that though they were tiring at times, I enjoyed them and found them full of interest. I have met with a great deal of friendliness and hospitality in America, and I content myself with retailing a few anecdotes, not as a basis for generalization but simply because they have stuck in my mind as unusual or unexpected.

In the course of my first American tour I travelled by plane from Boston to Dartmouth. The small plane was a hedge-hopper, in the sense that it flew very low and enabled one to see the countryside properly. I was enjoying the experience, when I noticed that a man sitting across the aisle was showing signs of excitement. Presently he asked me if I had seen a flying saucer going past. No, I replied, I had noticed no such object. The man got more and more excited and agitated, and in the end he made his way into the pilot's cabin to tell him all about it. I began to wonder whether we had a madman on board and what he proposed to do next. However, the stewardess succeeded in calming him down a bit, and we eventually landed safely at the modest airport at Dartmouth.

On another occasion I was flying back across the Atlantic and got into conversation with an elderly gentleman seated next to me. It transpired that he was of German origin, lived in California and had become a millionaire. He had no children, he told me, and was on his way to Berlin to inspect his relatives there and make up his mind whether any one of them was fit to be made his heir. I thought it a bit odd that a millionaire was travelling economy class. But my surprise ceased when a steward came round with drinks. The millionaire expressed to me the hope that the steward would forget to ask him to pay for his drink. When this in fact happened (I paid for mine), he was evidently delighted to have saved something in addition to what he had saved by travelling economy class. He was clearly no spendthrift, and I suspected that his relatives in Berlin would have to undergo a pretty rigorous inspection.

One summer (1968, I think) I was invited to take part in the East-West Philosophers Conference, at Honolulu, which took place every five years. As funds were available, largely provided by culturally interested local millionaires, for paying both travel and subsistence expenses of persons invited from outside the United States, I accepted with alacrity. The theme of this particular conference was alienation. At the time large or, at any rate, vociferous sections of university youth were conspicuous among the groups which liked to regard themselves as thoroughly alienated persons. And though the conference to which I had been invited was meant to bring together professional philosophers of East and West, students at the University of Hawaii were convinced that they had a right to express their complaints and ideas to the assembled philosophers. To be sure, if it had been a question simply of students from the Hawaiian islands, it is doubtful whether one would have heard a cheep from them. For the idyllic climate hardly encourages protest and energetic self-assertion. But there are, of course, many students from the mainland in the University of Hawaii, as well as students from the Far East. And some of these were doubtless determined to arouse their colleagues from their slumbers, and also the participants in the conference which was taking place on the Honolulu campus.

As it happened, a student agitator, an Indian, was visiting Hawaii on his rounds, and the university doubtless seemed to him in urgent need of an energetic troubling of the waters. When one evening his demands to be given the floor were granted, he treated the gathering of philosophers to an impassioned speech. Among other things he informed us in plain terms that we were a gang of hypocrites. At this vigorous sally the members of the conference loudly applauded. As the speaker evidently thought that the wind was being taken out of his sails, he reacted by adding some more broadsides and sweeping insults. However, as the philosophers took it all good-humoredly, the poor man, for all his vehemence, failed to create a scene.

On another evening of the conference the students were invited, in response to their request, to form a panel of their own, to take the place that evening of the ordinary academic panel of speakers, and they were told that they were free to say what they liked. The panel discoursed, as one would expect, about Vietnam, starving nations and such like topics. But the students had been so rash as to coopt onto the panel a youth who came from the city of Honolulu and who was said by some people to be a gang-leader. When the students on the panel had had their say, this youth was asked for his philosophy of life. He replied frankly and without frills that his philosophy of life was very simple; it consisted on looking first and foremost after Number One and if anyone got in his way, he would kick his face in. I felt rather sorry for the other members of the panel. For even if they thought that their hearers were a lot of old squares who should be put out to grass, they would certainly not subscribe to the philosophy of life stated by their comrade from the city. They were idealists, but he made it clear that he despised idealism.

Another anecdote. The United States Navy at Pearl Harbor had kindly invited the members of the congress to lunch and a tour of the scene of the sudden attack by the Japanese in the second world war. All was arranged, and a list of those proposing to avail themselves of the invitation was sent to the naval authorities. It included three Yugoslav professors and one philosopher from Czechoslovakia. This was too much for the naval authorities. On the day before the expedition to Pearl Harbor was to take place the Director of the conference, Professor Abe

Kaplan, was informed from Pearl Harbor that no flag officer of the U.S. Navy could sit down at lunch with a Communist. In other words, the philosophers from Communist countries must withdraw their acceptances. Professor
Kaplan replied that in this case nobody would go to Pearl
Harbor, and he would arrange for some other outing instead. After much discussion the Navy phoned the Director in the middle of the night to say that our Marxist colleagues could come after all, provided that they were content not to be placed at the admiral's table. So all was
well. After the tour of Pearl Harbor we were treated to
drinks, followed by an excellent lunch, and the officers
were most courteous and friendly. We were also shown
round a submarine (not nuclear, I imagine, though I
wouldn't know), given an exhibition of divers in a deep
tank, of the process of escaping from a sunk submarine,
and also treated to a film-lecture illustrating useful scientific research carried on by the U.S. Navy. A full day
and an interesting one.

Incidentally, the three Yugoslavs were very friendly
and open colleagues, while the Czechoslovak philosopher,
a quiet and amiable man, had to leave the conference
early, as he was summoned back to Prague and subsequently deprived of his chair by Dubcek's successors. It
is true that a couple of Russians had been invited and
had accepted, but at the last moment, when one of the or-
ganizers of the conference had already gone to the airport
to meet them, identical telegrams arrived to say that the
two men were unwell and unable to come.

Anyway, to show appreciation of the Navy's action in
changing its original refusal to accept guests from Communist countries Abe Kaplan published a report in a local
paper in which he warmly thanked the Navy for its
generous hospitality and praised its promotion of scientific research. The result of this was indignant protest
from those students who disapproved of anything being
said to the credit of the armed forces. Kaplan, however,
stuck to his guns, and rightly.

As one would obviously expect at an East-West philosophers conference, we had some Buddhist colleagues

from Japan. One evening we were addressed by the Japanese philosopher who was clearly regarded by his colleagues as their doyen and as the successor to Nishida. He started off in English. But it was extremely difficult to understand anything that he said, and he was politely offered an interpreter. He would have nothing to do with this suggestion. Presumably face would be lost if he had to speak in Japanese and rely on the services of an interpreter. So he continued throughout in what he believed to be English. At the end of his speech we all applauded, of course. But I had understood nothing, and I suspected from the evident difficulty experienced by the audience in finding a question to ask or a relevant comment to make that I was not alone in my lack of understanding.

One week I acted as chairman of the common or general sessions. This involved being publicly garlanded and chastely kissed on the first evening by a charming young lady. Besides this pleasant experience, however, the chairman for the week had the onerous task of trying to keep our Indian colleagues in order. I do not mean that the Indian philosophers were disorderly in the sense of making or causing rows. The situation was rather that an Indian professor rising to make what were supposed to be only a few brief remarks was only too likely not only to make a speech but also to hand the torch, so to speak, to another Indian, who would also make a speech. And so on. The chairman had to do his best to curtail the eloquence of his Indian colleagues. And some chairmen were not conspicuously successful. Even if the interventions made by the Indian philosophers were in themselves valuable contributions, there were other people who were waiting to put questions to the evening's panelists. And the chairman had to try to give them a chance to do so.

This chapter consists practically entirely of anecdotes, a fact which is likely to cause disappointment to any readers who were expecting to hear something about the author's general impressions and estimate of university life in the United States as compared with that in Britain. It seems to me preferable, however, to hold up any treatment of this subject until I come to say something about the time when I was spending considerable periods in America as a visiting professor after my retirement from the University of London in 1974. For during such periods I was obviously in constant contact with colleagues and with student classes and was thus somewhat better qualified to make comparative judgments about American and British university life than I was as a result of successive lecture-tours, when I was very much on the move.

Chapter 11

Some Radio Discussions

IN 1948 BERTRAND RUSSELL AND I DISCUSSED THE EXIST-
ence of God on the Third Programme of the BBC. How
many people had been invited by the BBC to debate with
Russell before I was approached, I do not know. Anyway,
having been invited, I rashly accepted. If I remember correctly, the topic, as originally stated by the BBC, was the
question whether the world was self-sufficient. It was
natural enough that Russell and I should have interpreted this as a question about the existence of God. At the
same time it is certainly arguable that we would have
done better to keep to the topic as originally formulated.
If it is asked whether God's existence can be proved, the
idea which tends to arise in the mind is that of asking
whether there is sufficient evidence that in addition to
stars, rocks, trees, animals, human beings, there is in the
universe an additional being called 'God,' a member of the
class of beings, a being 'out there.' This is hardly an adequate idea of God for an additional member of the class of
finite beings would not be what is meant by God, not at
any rate in the great monotheistic religions. The original
formulation of the topic for discussion or debate was less
likely to encourage this sort of idea. But it is doubtless
true that if Russell and I had spent all our time talking

about the concept of 'the world,' a good many listeners would have been disappointed.

On the appointed day I turned up in the foyer of Broadcasting House. Though I had not met Russell before, I immediately recognized him from his photographs. He was sitting in a corner, and I went up and introduced myself. In the course of conversation he expressed the hope that I would not introduce emotion into the debate. Whether he feared that I might call him a wicked man or that I would try to deliver an impassioned sermon, I did not ask. But when the debate was over, I was amused to find a reviewer saying that he preferred Russell's style to mine, as there was clearly an undercurrent of emotion or passion in what Russell had said, whereas I had been coldly rationalistic and detached. Russell thanked me for not having brought emotion into our discussion. I suppose that he thought that a religious believer, having a weak case from the point of view of reason, would be only too likely to indulge in emotive utterances. On occasion, however, Russell was himself much given to such utterances.

Anyway, Russell and I were set down on either side of a microphone and asked to get on with it. Finding myself confronted with an elderly philosopher with a worldwide reputation, I was naturally somewhat nervous. However, we managed to keep going, even if at one point it seemed that the discussion might dry up. What we said was supposed to be recorded by invisible machines, after which it would be typed, texts being sent to us for boiling down to the requisite length. As things turned out, the performance of the machines was defective, and we received texts interspersed with considerable blank spaces, with the request that we would reconstruct omitted passages in time for our next meeting, to be followed by the actual recording. As one might expect in the case of a relatively young and unknown person, I spent a good deal of time and trouble on reconstruction and, incidentally, in using what opportunities presented themselves for improving my position. Russell, however, did nothing at all. The result was that when we met on the appointed day,

Ordination group outside Heythrop College Chapel, 1937. Frederick Copleston standing in back row, extreme right. Rev. Thomas Williams, Archbishop of Birmingham, seated, front center.

Receiving an honorary doctorate at Creighton University,
Omaha, Nebraska, 1979. (Left: Rev. Matthew Creighton, S.J.)

Dr. S. K. Ookerjee, Rev. Frederick Copleston and Rev. A. Solagran outside the chapel at Wilson College, Bombay.

Receiving an honorary doctorate (Theology) at
the University of Uppsala, Sweden, 1983.

we had to work at the text all through lunch. Russell maintained that we were supposed to have parity of space, and that as, owing to my work of reconstruction, I had more material than he had, I should have to do most of the cutting. He admitted that he was to blame for not having attempted to reconstruct what was missing in his sections of the text, but he none the less expected me to do the cutting. Short of creating a scene, there was nothing to be done but for me to take a pencil and excise passages while trying to eat my lunch. Russell just modified a few of his statements. After lunch the agreed result was recorded.

The actual discussion fell into three parts. As a Catholic priest, especially in pre-Vatican II days, I was very conscious of what my correligionists and the ecclesiastical authorities might think about the positions which I adopted. I thought it incumbent on me to defend at any rate one traditional metaphysical line of proof of God's existence. My choice was acceptable to Russell, and in the first part of our debate we discussed such ideas as those of contingency and necessity and Leibniz's principle of sufficient reason. When I am asked nowadays what is my present opinion of the relevant line of argument, I am inclined to reply that the traditional *a posteriori* arguments for the existence of a transcendent reality have certain presuppositions, and that in any thorough discussion they should be made explicit and examined. To put the matter in another way, a formally valid argument for the existence of God is doubtless possible, given certain premises. But as the premises may be challenged, it is important to state and discuss them.

As for the second part of the debate, arguments from religious experience were not common, at any rate at the time, among Catholic theologians and philosophers. But I suppose that I introduced this line of thought under the impression that it would or might appeal to a number of listeners to whom talk about an absolutely necessary being would be pretty well unintelligible and probably irrelevant. If anyone is interested in reading my later reflections on arguments from religious experience in gene-

ral or from mystical experience in particular, let me refer
him or her to the fifth chapter of my *Religion and Philosophy* (1974) or to the ninth chapter of my Gifford lectures, *Religion and the One* (1982). Incidentally, I had the
impression that at any rate one reviewer of *Religion and
Philosophy* regarded what I had to say in the relevant
chapter as an expression of Thomist prejudice. I beg to
differ. What I said was the fruit not of any initial prejudice but of serious reflection on a particular line of argument.

In regard to the actual handling of the topic by Russell and myself, I confine myself to mentioning a misunderstanding which occurred in our original discussion.
Russell seemed to think that I was arguing from the
quality of the lives and characters of certain mystical
writers to the truth of their claims. But that was not
what I had in mind. The point which I wished to make
was simply that knowledge of a person's life and character may be sufficient to warrant the conclusion that he or
she sincerely believed what was said, and that the person
was not making claims which he or she knew or strongly
suspected to be bogus, out of a spirit of self-exaltation
and a desire for notoriety. In the text of the broadcast
there is indeed mention of this point, but, if I remember
correctly, a fuller explanation of my meaning was one of
the items which I struck out when reducing my material
to the amount required by parity of space.

The last part of the debate, on a moral argument to
the existence of God, seems to me pretty unsatisfactory.
In our original discussion I suggested to Russell that he
was really convinced that the policy of genocide pursued
by the Nazi government in regard to the Jews was wrong
in an absolute sense, and that even if, *ex hypothesi*, it
could be shown that the human race would be benefited
at some future date by the extermination of Jews at Aus-
chwitz and elsewhere, he would still condemn the extermination as wrong. Russell agreed, of course, that he
felt in this way. But he found some difficulty, he admitted, in squaring the implications of this admission with
his professed ethical theory. He even said something like

this. "I find myself in a dilemma. On the one hand I certainly want to condemn the Nazis' behavior towards the Jews as wrong in itself. On the other hand my ethical theory does not allow me to say this." When, however, it came to finalizing the text for broadcasting, Russell remarked that he could not say in public that he was in a dilemma, and he modified his admissions. Looking back on the debate, it now seems to me that part at any rate of Russell's ethical theory would permit him to condemn the Nazi policy of genocide absolutely. That is to say, in so far as he interpreted the moral judgment as expressing a subjective attitude, he could obviously condemn the policy. For he sincerely detested it. But I doubt whether his ethical theory would permit him to claim that the policy was wrong in itself, irrespective of how human beings might feel about it. The difficulty, it seems to me, lies in giving a fully satisfactory analysis of the meaning of 'in itself' in the context. But we were hardly able to give to this theme the consideration which it deserved.

Further, I would hesitate nowadays to argue directly, with Cardinal Newman, from the voice of conscience or from awareness (the feeling, as some would prefer to say) of moral obligation, of the categorical imperative, to the existence of God. What I have come to think is that in the development of the moral consciousness there can come a point at which it passes over into the religious consciousness, God being implicitly recognized (not necessarily explicitly) under the aspect of the good. But I admit that I have never thought the matter through to my own satisfaction. In any case I do not think that I would have got very far with Russell, if I had introduced this line of thought.

The story was told, at Oxford I think, that two undergraduates, one a theist, the other an atheist, listened to the debate, and that at the end the theist had become an atheist and the atheist a theist. The story is doubtless *ben trovato*. Moreover, it is probably true to say that such debates tend to leave people's beliefs what they were before. The fact that someone judges that one or other participant got the better of the contest does not neces-

138 / *Memoirs of a Philosopher*

sarily affect his or her personal beliefs in regard to the
substantial issue, here the existence of God. In other
words, the Copleston-Russell debate tended to be a performance, in regard to which listeners could award good
or bad marks to the participants as they thought fit. If
one were discussing God's existence with the sort of person who would genuinely like to believe but, for various
reasons, feels unable to do so or who does not really
know whether he or she believes or not, there might perhaps be real 'communication,' to borrow a term from Karl
Jaspers. But in confrontation with Bertrand Russell I
had the impression that each of us got down into his own
trench, so to speak, and sniped at the other over the par-
apet. Neither was going to change his position. It was a
question of who could snipe the more effectively, in the
estimation of the audience at any rate.

At one time I was sometimes invited to sit on a
panel of people who tried to answer questions submitted
by BBC listeners in European countries other than Great
Britain. On one of these occasions Bertrand Russell was
also a member of the panel. Some question about religious belief had been sent in, and the producer clearly
hoped and expected that Russell and I would engage in
combat. But I think that we both wished to avoid any
clash, and our remarks were hardly polemical in character. It seemed to me that the producer was disappointed
by our behavior.

In 1949 Professor (later Sir) Alfred J. Ayer and I discussed logical positivism on the Third Programme. From
one point of view this debate was easier for me than the
one with Russell. Ayer was, of course, well known as a
writer and broadcaster, but he was younger than I was,
and I had not got the feeling that I was debating with a
national monument. From another point of view, however, the discussion with Ayer was perhaps more wearing.
As everybody who knew him is well aware, Ayer had a
very quick mind and talked very rapidly, so that it was
difficult for a slowcoach like myself to keep up with him,
let alone think of a suitable reply or retort. Academi-
cally, I think that the Ayer-Copleston debate was superior

to the Copleston-Russell debate. But the subject obviously possessed much less popular appeal. Many people are prepared to express their ideas about the existence of God who have no idea of what logical positivism is or was.

The debate took place four years after the publication of the second edition of *Language, Truth and Logic*, in which Ayer had modified some of the things which he had said in the original 1935 edition. In 1949, however, logical positivism was still alive and had not yet been consigned to the history of philosophy, owing to the increasing dominance of somewhat different lines of thought. So I do not think that Ayer and I were discussing what was already a dead issue. In any case, even if logical positivism as a definite philosophy has since been subject to devastating criticism, it gave expression to a widespread outlook which is by no means dead. It is not unreasonable to see in logical positivism as expounded by the Vienna Circle and popularized by Ayer's famous book an attempt to provide a theoretical justification for a general outlook which both preceded and outlives the formal philosophy. Though they would be unlikely to express themselves in this abstract way, a good many people believe implicitly that to be or to exist is to be a possible (in principle) object of sense-perception, and logical positivism can be seen as attempting to justify theoretically this widespread implicit belief. True, it did not require a great deal of reflection to see that something must be wrong with logical positivism as presented in the first edition of *Language, Truth and Logic*. For example, the interpretation of historical statements was so eccentric that it could hardly win common acceptance. But when it is said that logical positivism is a past and long abandoned philosophy, it may be forgotten that it expressed an outlook which is by no means simply a thing of the past. Indeed, an inclination to flirt with this outlook can exist even in someone who is not prepared to throw metaphysics and theology out of the window as so much nonsense. For my part, while I believe that metaphysics is a legitimate and indeed indispensable part of philosophy, I am none the less aware in myself of a tendency to take a dim view of the cognitive value of speculative metaphysics. It is not simply a question of controversy with Ayer. I am also conscious of a dialogue with myself.

A few years later (I do not recollect the date) Ayer and I were invited to have a discussion on television. I think that it was a question of ITV. The subject suggested was faith. I told Ayer that I would prefer another subject, to which he retorted that if we did not discuss religion, he did not know what we were going to differ about. However, he accepted my suggestion that we should take a theme relating to the self. If he wished, he could defend the Humean analysis of the self, and I was prepared to defend the concept of the I-subject. So we settled on this topic.

Professor Ayer liked extempore discussion. As therefore we were asked to turn up at noon on the appointed day, the videotaping being fixed for 2:00 p.m., we not unnaturally assumed that we were going to be provided with lunch. Not a bit of it. We were treated to generous whiskies, a pre-lunch potation as we optimistically supposed. Then more whiskey. We were then told that there was no point in hanging about. As the videotaping machine was available, we had better go straight to the studio and do our stuff. On the way Ayer said to me, "I have never felt less combative in my life." I replied, "and I feel that I could not care less whether there is a self or not." The producer set us going, and after what seemed to me a few minutes I made a reference to theology. "I am afraid that we have no time for theology now," the producer broke in. I looked up at him with annoyance, thinking the remark unduly brusque and dismissive, when I suddenly realized that the whole half-hour had gone by, and that it was time to stop. I had very little idea of what either of us had said. "For heaven's sake, let's go and have some lunch," said Ayer. So we both repaired to a nearby restaurant.

A couple of weeks later the television company treated Ayer and myself to an excellent dinner in London, after which we were given a private showing of our performance. Visually, we both looked a bit odd. I had an inane grin on my face, which I was trying to wipe off with my hand. But the discussion seemed to me perfectly coherent. The trouble was that for a general television public it would be hardly intelligible. I recollect saying to Ayer, "You started by saying that there are five theories of the self and you proceeded to mention them in turn. What is the great British public going to make of that?" Ayer retorted, "Well, what about yourself? You were throwing about names such as Fichte as though they were household words in the British kitchen." I think that only two regional networks were prepared to put on the discussion.

The discussion just mentioned was a very amicable and good-natured affair. I remember a debate of a different sort with Mr. Rayner Heppenstall. In those days the Index of prohibited books, which Catholics were not supposed to read without due authorization, still existed, and the writings of Jean-Paul Sartre had just been added to it by Rome. Mr. Heppenstall and I were invited to discuss this event on radio. I assumed that after a more or less perfunctory reference to the Index we would give our attention to discussing Sartrean existenialism. After all, I knew that Heppenstall had published a book on existentialism. What I did not know, however, was that the Spanish Civil War had led him to take a very dim view of the Catholic Church and its doings. The discussion turned out to be a ding-dong battle of, to my mind, a rather absurd nature. Denunciations by Heppenstall of the Spanish Inquisition were countered on my part by charges that the record of certain Protestant countries in regard to credulous acceptance of the claims of witches and in regard to the ferocious treatment of the unfortunate ladies was worse than that of the Spanish Inquisition, which, on occasion, could show a certain healthy scepticism. Heppenstall even made the very odd suggestion (odd to anyone acquainted with Rome's ways) that Sartre's works had been put on the Index in order to increase the sale of Gabriel Marcel's writings. A good deal of heat and bad temper was engendered by the discussion, and I do not recollect anything of moment being said by either party about Sartre's philosophy, though it is, in my opinion, of considerable interest, even if analytic philosophers have been inclined to look askance at it or make it an object of ridicule. Obviously, Heppenstall was entitled to object to the institution of the Index (abolished, one may add, after Vatican II), but even if we were going to discuss this theme rather than Sartre's philosophy, our handling of the topic might profitably have been conducted on a higher intellectual plane. I am not, however, trying to put all the blame on Heppenstall's shoulders. I should not have let myself get involved in a profitless exhibition of polemics but should have insisted on keeping the discussion on a more respectable level.

The producers were amused and apparently pleased by the liveliness of the debate. To my relief, however, their superiors decided to pay us both our honoraria and not broadcast our altercation. Polemics of this sort are distasteful to me and tend to leave a bad taste in the mouth. For all I know, they may have been distasteful to Mr. Heppenstall also. That was, I think, the one and only occasion on which I met him, and I regret that it was not a more amicable encounter. As for the placing of Sartre's works on the Index, I very much doubt whether this made much, or any, difference to sales. I think that I am right in saying that the relevant Congregation in Rome did not usually add books to the Index, unless the writings in question had been officially drawn to their attention for examination and judgement. French traditionalist zealots were rather given to this practice, and the works of a good many French novelists and thinkers were on the Index. Germans, however, were much less given to this pastime, and, if I remember correctly, the works of Nietzsche did not appear in the Index, however strange this may appear.

In 1987 the BBC transmitted a series of interviews conducted by Bryan Magee with a number of philosophers, the texts of which formed the basis for chapters in the volume *The Great Philosophers* edited by Magee and published by BBC Books in the same year. I was invited by Magee to discuss with him the philosophy of Arthur Schopenhauer. There is little to say, however, about this series of broadcast discussions except that in my opinion, they admirably fulfilled the intended function of making the historical development of philosophical thought in the West more accessible to students not already well acquainted with it, including, of course, boys and girls in higher forms who were studying some philosophy. The series was in fact widely appreciated.

Some time during the period when I was teaching at the old Heythrop College in Oxfordshire, I had a radio discussion with Reg Butler, the sculptor. If I remember correctly, some notable people were asked whom they would like to meet for radio conversation, and Reg Butler said that he would like to meet me. So the BBC invited me. At the time I knew precious little about Butler's work (I do not mean to imply that I know much about it now), but he wanted, of course, to talk about aspects of religion, not about sculpture. I found him very pleasant, and we had an amicable conversation. I regret, however, that I remember very little, if anything about the content. I did possess a copy of what we said, but I think that in one of my changes of abode, usually preceded by extensive holocausts, I must have thrown out the relevant sheets. Anyway, I cannot find the text, and my memory remains pretty well a blank, apart from the uneasy feeling that I said little, if anything, of value and that I probably disappointed my partner in conversation or dialogue. I probably remember the occasion at all only because of Reg Butler's prominence in the art world.

Chapter 12

Two Eccentric Friends

IT WAS, I THINK, ON A SUNDAY AFTERNOON IN SEPTEM-ber 1951 that I was walking up the Grosser Scheidegg, enjoying the spectacle of the Jungfrau and the surrounding mountains, the clear air, the tinkle of the cattle-bells and other such amenities, when at a curve in the path I met a gentleman and lady coming down. The man looked a little uncertain, but said, "Aren't you the English priest who said Mass this morning in the church? I didn't recognize you at first in informal dress. You won't know me, of course, as I was just one of the congregation. My name is Fioravanti. This is Mrs. Green, who is staying with my nephew and myself in our chalet. I should be very pleased if you would come to dinner with us one day this week." So began a friendship which I greatly valued and of which I retain the warmest memories.

At that time at any rate hotels in that part of Switzerland cooperated in a scheme for providing for the religious needs of foreign tourists during the summer season. At Wengen there was a Catholic church or chapel which was ordinarily served, on some Sundays at least, by a Franciscan who came from a considerable distance and who catered for the needs of the few local Catholics. During the summer season, however, one of the hotels was prepared to provide basic board and lodging for an

English-speaking priest, provided that he paid his own fare to Wengen and back. Apart from saying two Masses on Sundays and hearing confessions, he was free to take a holiday. In the summer in question I had taken on a period of three weeks at the tail end of the tourist season. In point of fact there were no English-speaking Catholic tourists left, and I preached in my defective German.

As the season was pretty well over and the hotel was waiting to shut up shop until the winter season arrived, I felt that I was there rather on sufferance, simply because existing arrangements had better be respected. The young Italian waiter who served my meals was a simple and friendly youth, and the Swiss Catholic lady who looked after the chapel was glad of an occasional chat. But in the absence of any English-speaking tourists I was pretty well entirely on my own. Sunday morning was rather trying, as the two Masses were separated by an interval of three hours, and in those days one could not even have a cup of coffee after the early Mass. Apart, however, from Sunday mornings I was left to my own devices. The walks, of course, were delightful, but I got tired of my own company. It was thus a real pleasure when Valdemaro Fioravanti spoke to me on that Sunday afternoon and invited me to his chalet.

Valdemaro lived at Florence. But he had an apartment at Bern and a chalet at Wengen. He liked to spend some months during the summer in Switzerland, when he was visiting his multitudinous friends in various countries. He was extremely hospitable and invited all sorts of people to stay with him, with the result that sometimes beds had to be made up on the floor. At the moment when I first met him, however, his only guest in the chalet, apart from his nephew, was the lady mentioned above, the wife of a retired naval officer. Valdemaro had met them both in England, and the wife was staying with him while waiting for her husband to join her on the continent. The nephew, then a boy of fifteen or so, was a pupil at an international school at Lausanne and generally came to the chalet at Wengen for week ends. During my stay at Wengen I saw a lot of Valdemaro and his nephew, not only at meals in the chalet but also on expeditions. The cooking in the chalet was done by Valdemaro, and very well, even if punctuality was definitely not one of his virtues.

Both Valdemaro and his nephew spoke fluent English. The nephew, though somewhat given to moods, was a nice boy. His father, a Duke with estates in Sicily, whom I was to meet at Florence, was an ardent Anglophile, who spoke English by preference, whenever the opportunity occurred. He had been educated at English public school (Cheltenham, I think), and during the second world war he was commandant of a POW camp for officers. He had evidently done his best for the prisoners under his command, for when they held reunion dinners after the war they always invited their former commandant to be their guest, an invitation which he accepted with alacrity and of which he was very proud. As for his son, Valdemaro's nephew, after school he became a driver of fast cars for some international firm. It was hoped that he would marry happily and settle down in Italy. But he died at an early age in somewhat mysterious circumstances on Majorca or Minorca, I forget which. When I was at Wengen, he was a lively boy, full of fun, except when he was in one of his black moods.

Valdemaro was such a spontaneously friendly and open human being that it was very easy to get on with him. On occasion he could become irritated and angry, but his feelings of annoyance quickly passed. Though a man of deep religious conviction and high moral ideals, he was extremely tolerant of people's failings, at any rate in the area of sexual behaviour, and he told stories about them with such innocent gusto that even the perhaps somewhat staid English lady who was his guest for the first week or so of my stay at Wengen had to laugh. On one occasion she said to me, "You know, I don't think that Valdemaro at all realizes what he is saying; he just sees the funny side of things." I think that this about summed up the situation.

My new friend was pressing in his invitations to me to stay with him at Florence. At the time I did not see how this would be feasible. But when the next year I started lecturing at Rome for part of each year, it became possible to break the journey at Florence. At first I was somewhat apprehensive. Valdemaro was always filling the house, where his mother lived, with guests from all over the place, and I had the impression that the Marchesa found it too much of a good thing. When Valdemaro related to me how on one occasion his mother and he had smashed all the breakfast things to express their feelings at the moment, I wondered what I had let myself in for. Besides I was none too confident that the Marchesa would relish having a foreign priest to help entertain. Fortunately, she and I got on excellently. In a sense we got on too well for Valdemaro's taste. For as the years went by he began to think that his mother was making a point of trying to annex his friends and enlist their sympathy. I doubt this very much, in my case at least. I think she just found me a peaceable sort of person, with whom she could talk quietly about things which interested her. She read a good deal and liked to discuss what she read, whereas her son was always on the go.

The Fiorovanti's house at Florence was up at Bellosguardo, on the other side of the city from Fiesole, and with a magnificent view over the valley. In the mornings, when I looked out of my window, I saw Brunelleschi's dome rising out of the mist. At sunset the whole city glowed, and the purple hills or mountains were a sight of which I never tired. The estate was fairly large, with vineyards and olive orchards. In the summer Valdemaro often obtained extra help by letting wandering students take up residence in one of the cottages in the grounds. In return for board and lodging they worked at whatever task needed to be done at the time. Valdemaro often asked them up for meals at the main house, and sometimes he had a student staying for a while in the house itself. On one occasion, I remember that there was a youth of about seventeen from New Zealand, who had worked his passage in a ship's galley and had then taken jobs in a number of countries. He was seeing the world, and after working in Italy he planned to go on to North Africa or Egypt. I hardly thought this wise. Nor did Valdemaro. But whether we succeeded in dissuading him I don't know. His project of seeking casual work in Muslim countries seemed to me highly imprudent, though my apprehensions, shared by Valdemaro, may possibly have been groundless.

This particular youth helped Valdemaro for a time with his animals. The number of living creatures on the estate grew constantly, until there must have been more than two hundred of them. There were rabbits, silver pheasants, birds of all sorts, hens and chickens, dogs, cats, sheep, tortoises, ducks, geese, turkeys and heaven knows what not. When I first visited Valdmaro at Florence, the situation was not so bad as it later became. The number of birds and animals was less; Valdemaro had help in feeding the creatures; and now and then he had time to make expeditions with his guests. Later, however, care for the vast menageries came to demand so much attention that Valdemaro would go out in the middle of meals to look after the creatures, and there was little time left for any other activity. In other words, care for his animals and birds grew into a kind of mania. Thus during the night I became aware of strange noises and rustlings and movements through the wall. I discovered that sick rabbits, hens and so on were transferred from the garden to an adjoining room, and that Valdemaro ministered to them at all hours of the day and night.

At Wengen Valdemaro had told me that he had a living crocodile at Florence. Naturally I asked him if I could see the creature, when I visited him at Florence. "It is in the room next to you. Come and see." I was taken into the room, the sheets on the bed were pulled back, and there lay a large reptile, with its head on the pillow. I hasten to add that it was no longer alive. During one of Valdemaro's absences from Florence, the creature had apparently not been looked after properly and had died. Valdemaro had had it embalmed, and it now lay in state.

The growing preoccupation on Valdemaro's part with his menageries seemed to me to set up a kind of vicious circle. He professed to want a wife very much. But she must fulfill four conditions. She must be Catholic, she must be English, she must come of an aristocratic family, and she must be fond of animals. I was asked for suggestions. Not moving in aristocratic society, I was of little help. Anyway, I am inclined to think that preoccupation with the menagerie was partly the result of failing to find the desired wife. At the same time the more the preoccupation grew, the less likely did it become that any suitable lady would be willing to marry Valdemaro. Affection for a pet dog or two or an interest in horses is one thing. To have birds flying about your bedroom and to have a husband who absents himself for hours at a time to care for sick rabbits and hens or feed a growing menagerie is another matter.

The menageries included some sheep. As far as I could ascertain, they lived in some room on the ground floor and were let out in the morning to mow a lawn. That is to say, they pursued their grass-eating activities in a movable wire cage, the location of which on the grass remained unchanged until they had done their job properly. On my last visit before Valdemaro's death he had invited an Austrian Archduke and his wife to lunch. After lunch I was strolling in the garden with the Archduchess, a charming German lady, and having come to the conclusion that the sheep needed some fresh grass, we pushed the cage on. Hardly had we done so than Valdemaro's head appeared from a window, and the Archduchess and I were soundly rebuked for our interference.

The animal question was one of the bones of contention between son and mother, especially when the Marchesa had been ill and subject to bouts of depression. She would wring her hands and repeat that she did not know what would become of them all. One evening a Venetian nobleman and his wife came to dinner. After dinner the Venetian took the opportunity of cornering me alone (Valdemaro, needless to say, was feeding the menagerie) to read me a lecture on my duty to take the Marchesa's part and persuade Valdemaro to get rid of the animals and devote himself to looking after his mother and the estate. I dare say that the Venetian guest was quite right in what he said, but I did not feel that Valdemaro was likely to pay heed to any moral lecture from myself. Besides, at the time it was very difficult to get hold of Valdemaro for serious conversation. The servants were either ill with influenza or away looking after sick relatives, and Valdemaro was dividing the time between the kitchen and the animals. It did not seem a very propitious time for preaching him a sermon. Knowing Valdemaro, I thought that any action would be likely to cause an explosion. So I decided to postpone taking any steps until the domestic staff was well again and my host was a little less overburdened with work. As things turned out, however, this was my last visit. I have regretted my failure to say more to Valdemaro while there was still a chance of his paying some attention, but I am inclined to think that by the time the guest from Venice exhorted me to take action Valdemaro was too much in the grip of his fixation of rescuing and caring for stray animals for anything that I could say to make much difference to his conduct.

By the time of his death the animals and birds on his estate had become the focus of Valdemaro's life. He rose at some unearthly hour to look after them, and in the end he got little sleep. Sometimes at night he would find a letter which he ought to have read long before, start to read it and then fall asleep exhausted in a chair before he had taken in more than a few lines. He was no longer young, being a little older than myself, and he had already had what appeared to be heart trouble. I think that it was early in 1969, when I was in hospital at Oxford recovering from an operation, that my brother, kindly visiting me from London, drew my attention to a notice of Valdemaro's death which had appeared in *The Times*. Later on I learned what had happened. Valdemaro had been feeling ill. The doctor had paid a visit and had told him to go straight to bed and stay there. Directly he heard the noise of the doctor's car on the gravel of the drive, as the doctor departed, Valdemaro got out of bed, dressed and started out in his car to go down into the city to fetch feeding-stuff for his animals. When he turned into the road leading to the city, he felt very ill and stopped at the parish priest's house to ask for a glass of water. After a chat with the priest he felt somewhat better, said goodbye and moved towards his car. Between the priest's house and the car he fell to the ground dead.

No doubt this was the sort of death for which Valdemaro would have wished. But it was a great shock to his many friends. For my own part, I have subsequently avoided Florence. When complications consequent on my operation arose, my superiors told me to take a holiday, and after Easter I flew to Rome and then worked my way slowly up Italy, visiting places which were new to me, such as Spoleto and Vicenza. But I carefully avoided even passing through Florence. The memories of happy hours at Valdemaro's house and of expeditions with him and his friends were too vivid in my memory.

What I have been saying about Valdemaro's menagerie may have given the impression that he was a monomaniac, who had lost his sense of humour and feeling for other human beings. This, however, would be a very one-sided impression. I look back with pleasure to the visits which I paid to Bellosquardo before a bit of eccentricity had been succeeded by or developed into what threatened to become an all-engrossing fixation. In the morning we would walk together through an olive orchard, pass through a door in a wall and go a little way down a lane to the local church, where I would say Mass. Afterwards we breakfasted together on a terrace. The Marchesa was still in her room. Valdemaro was lively at breakfast and imparted bits of Florentine gossip and scandal in a most humorous way. He then went off to see to his animals, of which there were at the time only a fairly reasonable number. Later he was ready for going into the city or making an expedition. I well remember visits to Tuscan hill towns with Valdemaro and the English, Belgian or Hungarian art students whom he had got to know. (They generally belonged to families with which Valdemaro was well acquainted). Then there were various social gatherings in houses near Florence. And Valdemaro himself had, as already mentioned, a succession of guests. After dinner he had the habit of dropping off to sleep in the middle of a conversation and snoring loudly. As people were used to this behaviour, nobody took any notice. After a while Valdemaro would wake up and become very animated.

On one occasion Valdemaro, who had by then got hold of a rather ramshackle car, took me to dine with a certain wine-producing Baron who had a castle in the Apennines. We took country roads, and the views of the mountains and valleys were superb. After an enjoyable drive we arrived at a formidable looking castle. The Baron was not to be seen. There was some lawsuit going on between him and one of Valdemaro's in-laws, and he (the Baron) was taking his meal privately. We were lavishly entertained, however, by the female members of the family. When at last we left, Valdemaro, who was not in any case one of the world's first-class drivers, shied at the thought of going back the way we had come and announced that we would make for Siena, where we could take a main road back to Florence. We lost our way, but eventually we arrived at Siena, where we drank hot chocolate in the Piazza in the middle of the night. On the main road our progress was slow, for the lights of oncoming cars dazzled Valdemaro and made him very nervous. He therefore stopped at frequent intervals and had a nap, while I had to twiddle my thumbs or pray. It was morning when we reached home.

On another occasion Valdemaro informed me that we had been invited to tea by a gentleman who lived in the vicinity of Lucca. By this time the animal mania had started to grow, and Valdemaro spent so long with the creatures that it was already time for tea when he at length said that he was ready to start. Although it was so late, he was determined to go. An old fellow in his

eighties had just married a girl of seventeen. Both were
to be present at tea, and Valdemaro thought that it
would be amusing to meet them. So off we started, only
to get lost on the way. Valdemaro accordingly parked the
car, with me in it, right in the middle of a main road and
went off to seek directions at a filling-station, which lay
behind us. Cars whizzed by, causing the ancient vehicle
in which I was sitting to shake like a decrepit boat in a
storm. After about half an hour Valdemaro returned, and
we proceeded on our way. When we eventually reached
the gentleman's house, all the guests had long since departed. We were given a drink, however, and Valdemaro,
looking mischievously at me the while, let fall a series of
strong, not to say obvious, hints that we had not yet
dined and would be glad to do so. The gentleman, who
had evidently already dined by the time of our arrival, ig-
nored the hints. In the end even Valdemaro had to accept defeat, and we went off to Lucca to get some supper
in a restaurant. The return journey to Florence was
punctuated, as usual, by frequent stops for Valdemaro to
take a nap.

Valdemaro was so unaffected and open-hearted that
he could get on excellently with people in pretty well any
walk of life. At the same time he had a curiously exalted
notion of the vocation of the aristocracy, by which I think
he meant not only the aristocracy in the customary English sense of the word but also what used to be called
the gentry. He was not, of course, under any illusion
about the goings-on of some of the bearers of famous
names among the Italian nobility, but he regarded them
as failing to live up to the aristocracy's God-given vocation of setting a good example to lesser mortals. His
mother the old Marchesa, who was of Swiss origin, remarked to me once that Valdemaro did not understand or
could not bring himself to accept the truth that the aristocracy counted for little in the modern world. This was
doubtless true. None the less there was something delightfully old-world in his attitude. He had become a
Knight of Malta and was intensely proud of it, looking on
his membership as a real religious vocation.

His attitude to the aristocracy was accompanied by a persistent loyalty to the royal family of Italy. One soon learned not to refer for example, to the 'ex-king.' One would be told that there was no 'ex' about it. His Majesty was still King of Italy, and if he was temporarily unable to exercise the functions of his position, this did not mean that he was no longer the sovereign. Incidentally, Valdemaro bore some resemblance to the ex-king, and he liked to relate how once a gentleman sitting in the same train compartment plucked up the courage to say, "Pardon me, Your Majesty, but should you be travelling alone?"

In my opinion, Valdemaro's exalted idea of the vocation of the aristocracy, his respect for the throne and its occupant (whether actual or 'ex'), his veneration for the Knights of Malta as a relgious order, were all expressions of a strong sense of the embodiment of the sacred in traditional institutions. So, I think, was his attitude to a priest in the working-class suburbs of Florence, who was on remarkably good terms with the local Communists. It is probably true to say that most of his parishioners voted Communist, especially in the municipal elections, a line of action which was highly disapproved of by the Holy See and the Italian bishops. The priest in question obviously believed that it was his duty as having charge of a parish to approach those of his potential flock who were alienated from the Church and those who would like to combine left-wing politics with religion. He himself, of course, was a sincere adherent of left-wing convictions and felt strongly in sympathy with the workers. Otherwise he would hardly have succeeded in winning their confidence. As things turned out, he filled his church. But his friendly relations with Communists and his tolerance of *Unita,* the Communist daily, being sold outside the church, aroused the marked displeasure of the austere Archbishop of Florence of that time. In the end, I think, the Archbishop 'suspended' the priest in question from the exercise of his priestly functions and sent a priest from the cathedral to say Mass in the church on Sunday. The male parishioners, however, formed a cordon in front of the altar, and the visiting priest, being unable to approach the altar, had to return to the cathedral. Needless to say, the saga was discussed in the Italian papers, and there was a fine scandal. Valdemaro's attitude was simple. As far as he was concerned, the offending priest was guilty of disobedience to the powers ordained by God, and that was that. Had not the Holy See and the Italian bishops made it clear that Catholicism and Communism were incompatible? Valdemaro was not impressed by arguments to the effect that the priest was a man who faced up to the realities of life and was trying to bring the Christian message to the workers. The priest may have had good intentions, but his clear obligation, in Valdemaro's eyes, was to follow the directions of the Archbishop, the superior placed over him by God.

Obviously, Valdemaro was not personally involved in the course of events; he was simply an observer. But as I have dwelt at some length on his growing preoccupation with caring for his menagerie and with constantly adding to it stray dogs, wounded birds and such like, I wanted to draw attention to one or two other aspects of his scale of values and outlook on the world.

I have left myself little space for saying something about another somewhat eccentric friend, Lady Boynton, Naomi as she invited me to call her. My first meeting with her was in Rome. After a lecture which I had given in the British Council Institute she invited Mr. Kennedy-Cooke, the then Representative of the British Council in Italy, and myself to drinks at her hotel. Both of us accepted. Little did I know at the time what I was letting myself in for.

Naomi had a flat in London, and she pressed me to let her know when I would be in London, so that she could ask me to a meal. At the time Heythrop College in Oxfordshire was my base in England, and now and again I visited London, to give a lecture or attend a meeting. Sometimes, of course, I did not tell Naomi of my visit, but if she knew that I would be available, she would invite me to a meal, in her flat perhaps, if there were no guests, otherwise in a hotel restaurant. As she was ac-

customed to choose first-class hotels and entertain lavishly, I naturally assumed that she was a wealthy
woman. She was married to a retired naval commander,
who seemed to have a strong sympathy with Buddhism
and whose main topic of conversation, according to his
wife, was cars, preferably fast ones. I met him and liked
him, but during the years of my acquaintanceship with
Lady Boynton I saw little of him. He seemed to spend
his time either at his club in London or on the family estate in Yorkshire, and I gathered that husband and wife
were accustomed to going their different ways. When he
died, however, I was asked to celebrate the Requiem
Mass at Farm Street church.

On one occasion when I lunched with Naomi in her
flat, I remember that the old retainer, a devout lady who
frequented the Brompton Oratory, brought in the potted
shrimps, humming the while. As Naomi was also given
to humming, at any rate if there any break in the conversation, she proceeded to join in. Not to be left out, I also
began humming. And there were the three of us all merrily humming away.

When Naomi entertained in hotels, the guests whom
I encountered tended to be the same. Thus I several
times met Dame Marie Rambert, June Lady Audley, one
of Lord Curzon's daughters, and Lady Listowel, who had
much of interest to say about her travels. As for Rome,
Naomi liked to be there for a while during the winter, as
she had a number of friends there, such as the Marchesa
Maria Cristina Marconi, Prince and Princess Castelbanco,
the Marchesa de la Gandara (lady-in waiting to the ex-
Queen of Spain) and the Conte and Contessa Della Rocca.
The Countess had been a lady-in-waiting to the Queen of
Italy, while the Count was a staunch supporter of the
Italian Liberal Party. Thus when Naomi was in Rome, I
met some members of the nobility as fellow guests, but,
needless to say, I came across them only through Naomi
and because she pressured me into coming along. In one
sense, however, I foolishly allowed myself to be turned
into a kind of special retainer. Whereas Naomi allowed
other guests, both in London and Rome, to depart in

peace when they started making their farewells, I was expected to stop on after they had gone and keep Naomi company for a while.

Naomi was a great storyteller, and over the period when I knew her I heard a good many of her tales. These were told as historical facts, but I soon found that one had to make up one's own mind about the dosage of truth which they might contain. Naomi did not usually give me an account of her doings when I could hardly fail to see its falsity, gullible though I might be. For example, one summer I learned, though not from Naomi, that she had been telling people in Rome how she had been involved in the recent terrible Valjont dam disaster in northern Italy and how she had ministered to the stricken families. If she never told me this story, it was presumably because she very well knew that we had both been in Florence at the time, that she had taken me to call on the famous conductor Signor Gui, and that the first either of us had heard of the dam disaster was from Madam Gui, who informed us that all theatres were shut that day in Florence, as news of the disaster had just arrived. Sometimes, however, Naomi did treat me to a story which she can hardly have expected me to regard as factual. Once she related to me how she had suffered a heart attack on a plane, and that the steward, reluctant to have a sick person on board, had got rid of her through a window. When she came to on the ground, she heard a passing peasant talking French and thus knew in what country she had landed. She told the story with such gusto that one could enjoy it as imaginative fiction. Whether Naomi believed any of it, I really do not know.

Sometimes, of course, Naomi related tall stories which either certainly or probably or possibly had some sort of basis in fact, a basis on which a superstructure of fiction had been erected. The difficulty generally was to detect the basis, though from one point of view it mattered little. That is to say, as long as one had not got to *do* anything which presupposed belief in the story, one could simply take the whole thing as amusing fiction. If, however, some personal action was required, the situation was different. Let me illustrate each type of story.

One of Naomi's prize stories was her account of how she had swum the Danube to rescue priests out of Communist Hungary. After swimming the river, she spent two or three days in a cemetery, occupying an empty tomb, then contacted several priests and brought them safely into Austria. On her reporting her exploits to Pope Pius XII, the Pope, while commending her zeal, asked her not to repeat the performance, as priests should stay with their flocks and not flee the country when confronted with difficulties in pursuing their vocation.

Though Pius XII might well have discouraged Naomi from depriving Hungary of its priests, if she had really been acting in this way, it was obvious that most of the story was fiction. Was there any basis of truth at all? It occurred to me that as Naomi was certainly acquainted with members of an aristocratic Austrian family with estates near the frontier, it was possible that at some time after the war she had stayed with the family, had heard stories about escapes from Soviet satellite countries, and had created the rest of her tale out of her fertile imagination. As, however, the issue had no practical relevance for me, I never tried to locate the element of truth in the story, if, indeed, there was any such element.

On another occasion Naomi told me a story which led to my finding myself in a rather embarrassing situation. Part of what she said was true enough. When years before, she had been a pupil at a well known convent school near London, she had had a Portuguese friend who had later married the Duke of Palmella. The Duke had been Portuguese ambassador in London during the second world war and had many English friends. After the war he and his wife generally came over in the late summer and stayed for a while at Claridge's, where they were able to entertain. One day Naomi took me along to dine with the Palmellas. They were very gracious, and it was obviously true that the Duchess and Naomi had been at school together. Though, however, I had just met them in the way described, I was very surprised when, at

a later date, Naomi assured me that the Duke and Duchess were anxious that I should stay with them in their
mansion in Lisbon on the occasion of my lecturing-tour
for the British Council in 1964. For I had been told by
someone that to get into the Palmellas' house in Lisbon
was like trying to get access to Buckingham Palace.
However, I was aware that Father C.C. Martindale had
once been invited to stay with the Palmellas with a view
to writing a book on the shrine at Fatima, and also that
the Duke kept up relations with his old school in England, Beaumont College near Windsor, which was run by
the Jesuits. I could not, therefore, altogether exclude the
possibility that Naomi had been telling the truth, when
she said that I had been invited to accept hospitality
from the Palmellas during the Portuguese part of my lecture-tour. After repeated assurances from Naomi that
this was in fact the case, I wrote to the Duke and expressed my appreciation of his kindness, at the same
time pointing out that the Portuguese Jesuits in Lisbon
might expect me to stay with them while I was in the
city. The Duke replied that his wife and he certainly
wished to have me as their guest, and that he had had a
word with the Portuguese Jesuit Provincial, who was very
glad that I should accept the Palmellas' invitation. On receiving this letter I accepted without further hesitation,
and the Palmellas, needless to say, were perfect hosts
and made my stay a very pleasant memory for me. At
the same time I have often wondered since whether
Naomi had not imagined the invitation and whether she
had not, in effect, placed the Palmellas in a position
where their profound Catholic devotion and their respect
for the English Jesuits, not to speak of their natural
courtesy, left them little choice but to receive me as a
guest in their house. The more that I came to understand that Naomi's assurances could by no means always
be taken at their face-value, the more was I inclined to
suspect that I had been foisted by her on the Palmellas.
Suspicions of this kind may appear neurotic to anyone
unacquainted with Naomi and her ways. But experience
suggested otherwise.

As already related, for a good many years I used to travel out to Rome for the beginning of the first semester of the academic year in October, returning to England in the course of February. These journeys gave Naomi an opportunity to exercise her ingenuity in lighting on ways to realize her wishes. This was the kind of thing. One year Naomi had tried to persuade me to accompany her during the summer vacation to the north of England. The programme, I was given to understand, was to make a kind of triumphal progress by car, staying with various important people on the way, and to end up at her husband's ancestral mansion where we would spend some weeks. I did not relish the thought either of being foisted as a doubtless unwelcome guest (and also unwilling one) on a series of county families or of spending several weeks dancing attendance on Naomi in the seclusion of the northern countryside. So I made excuses. "But you must take a holiday," said Naomi. I replied that this had been taken care of. With due permission of my Superior I had arranged to take a short holiday in Italy on the way back to Rome. For the time being Naomi left matters there. Later on, at a meeting in London, she said: "It's a very tiring train journey to Rome. And I know you; you will go second class without a sleeper. You'll be tired out. You can't do it." Unwisely I replied that I proposed to take a plane to Milan and start my holiday from there. Again Naomi dropped the subject. On a later occasion she said something like, "You told me that you were flying to Milan on September 18th." Like a fool I fell into the trap and replied, "No, I'm flying on the 20th." At which Naomi triumphantly exclaimed, "I shall be there to meet you, and we can take a bit of holiday together." I had let myself be manoeuvred into a position in which I had a choice between being thoroughly rude or capitulating. I capitulated.

If I say that this sort of thing happened more than once, I probably give the impression of suffering from a signal lack of will-power. It was pretty obvious that Naomi wanted a travel companion, that she found difficulty in finding one, and that she saw me as a kind of

gift from heaven, as someone who would be patient enough to sit and chat with her over drinks and who, as a
priest who was accustomed to saying Mass every morning, would act as a kind of chaplain. If travelling with
Naomi and acting as companion and chaplain for the duration was repugnant to me, why did I not resolutely refuse to take the job on?

I think that the answer, or a large part of it, is that
though I certainly felt exasperated from time to time and
blamed myself for my folly in letting myself in for acting
as a travelling companion, there were none the less aspects of the situation which I liked and would be reluctant to forego. Naomi was accustomed to play the *grande
dame* and carry on as if expense was of no concern to her.
A journey to Rome became much more attractive if on the
way one could visit attractive places in comfort, such as
Rocadamour, Carcassonne, Aix-en-Provence, Sirmione on
the Lago di Garda, and so on. I already had my basic
ticket, so to speak, and if I raised questions about the expense involved by divagations and staying in first-class
hotels, my queries were simply brushed aside as unneces-
sary and irrelevant. Besides, though there were certainly
times when dancing attendance on Naomi was extremely
irksome, she could be and often was an amusing and
lively companion, with a strong sense of humour and a
fund of stories, some mainly or partly true, others imaginative fiction. Looking back on my travel experiences
with her, I do not find myself wishing that they had
never taken place. They certainly put some unusual col-
our into my life.

In the political area Naomi had no use at all for so-
cialism and seemed incapable of appreciating socialist ideals. In regard to religion, she was a practising Catholic,
but she was repelled by changes introduced into the
Church after Vatican II. For example, the use of the vernacular at Mass was to her an abomination. In other
words she liked what she had been brought up to value
and had no intention of changing either her political or
her religious ideas. In conversation with her I tried to

keep off such topics. There was really no point in either of us getting unnecessarily irritated.

Naomi's heyday must have been before I came to know her, and I think that it was largely consciousness of the fact that she had already had her fling, so to speak, which impelled her to grasp at a straw, to take up a priest immersed in the academic life and make of him a travelling companion, when this was practically possible. After her husband's death she retired to a hospital where she spent a good many years before dying at an advanced age. For a time I visited her fairly regularly, as opportunity offered, but when she had ceased to recognize people and lived in a world of her own, there seemed little point in continuing the practice. After her death, however, I said a Requiem Mass for her in London at the request of relatives. I like to remember her in her days of activity, of course, not as she was in the unhappy years after her husband's death.

Chapter 13

From the Cotswolds to London

THE LAST CHAPTER, TOGETHER WITH CHAPTER TEN, MAY have given the impression that I spent most of my time travelling abroad in various countries. In actual fact, however, the greater part of each year was passed in studying, writing and lecturing either at Heythrop College in Oxfordshire or at the Gregorian University in Rome. At Heythrop the number of my external social engagements was negligible. At Rome the number was somewhat greater, but I kept it to the minimum compatible with good manners, and Naomi Boynton's tendency to turn up suddenly on the Roman scene, phone me from her hotel and pretty well demand that I should drop whatever I was doing and appear for a meal was one of the features of her conduct which exasperated me. As for my occasional travels with her and my visits to Valdemaro Fioravanti at Florence, these took place in connection with journeys out to or back from Rome, not during the actual semesters of the academic year. They provided a periodic relief from the routine of lecturing and writing, and I was certainly self-centred enough to regard them as such.

At the close of chapter eight mention was made of the move of Heythrop College from the Cotswolds to London in the summer of 1970, when the College started to occupy the building of the former postgraduate College of Education in Cavendish Square which had been vacated by the Holy Child nuns. Inasmuch as the bulk of the staff and student body of the College, together, of course, with the extensive library, were transferred from Oxfordshire to the new location in London, there was obviously a real element of continuity, and it is natural to speak of the College moving from one site to another, especially as we retained the name 'Heythrop College.' Technically, however, Heythrop in London was a new College. Well before the move took place, the University of London had insisted that application should be made in due form to the Queen in Council for the establishment within Greater London of a University College to be known as 'Heythrop College,' for purposes specified in the Charter. The Royal Charter was actually granted on May 14, 1971. Thereupon the University accepted Heythrop College as a non-grant-receiving College of the University for a probationary period of five years. The College was recognized in the first instance as a School in the Faculty of Theology, and in June 1974 it was admitted to the Faculty of Arts for the purpose of preparing students for degrees involving philosophy. At the end of the five-year period the Senate granted the College permanent status as a non-grant-receiving School of the University of London. It would thus be quite incorrect to suppose that the University took to its bosom the Pontifical Athenaeum, conferring ecclesiastical degrees in accordance with regulations laid down by Rome. The University insisted that if the Pontifical Athenaeum were to continue its existence in London, it must do so as a separate and independent entity. The new Heythrop College would not confer pontifical degrees; it would prepare students for degrees and diplomas of the University of London, like any other School of the University.

According to the First Schedule of the Charter, the first Principal of the new College should be myself. I was thus faced for the first time in my life with a serious administrative responsibility. To be sure, I had been Dean of Philosophy in the Pontifical Athenaeum, but this was no great burden. In London the situation was different. The College was juridically a new foundation; we were feeling our way; and there were among us different views of the way in which the College should develop. Growing pains were inevitable. Happily I received invaluable advice and support from the then chairman of the governing body of the College, Professor D.W. Hamlyn of Birkbeck College. I have no doubt that I bothered him with problems which I should have been able to solve through my own efforts, but I have never forgotten his patience with my importunities, and I feel very grateful to him for his interest in the fledgling College and for the way in which, as chairman of the governing body, he helped to guide Heythrop through its first years.

In 1972 the Senate conferred on me the personal title of 'professor of the history of philosophy,' and in the same year the Faculty of Theology did me the honour of electing me as Dean, a post which I held until I retired from the University in 1974. My various relations with the University were a source of pleasure to me, but I had my difficulties within the College, not, indeed, with the students, but with colleagues. Looking back, I think that I perhaps made a mistake in trying to combine being Principal with writing. I had obviously been appointed the first Principal of the College not because of any proven administrative ability but because within a limited academic circle my name was known as a writer on philosophical topics, and during my time as Principal I tried to get in what writing I could. Given, however, my inexperience in administration, I think that it might have been better if I had abandoned writing for the duration and given more prolonged attention to internal politics. It might perhaps be suggested that instead of involving myself in administrative duties I would have done better to avoid the nomination as first Principal of the College. But my Jesuit Superiors were keen on my taking up the job, and I can quite understand the reason. To preside over the infancy of the new College they wanted to find someone whose name was not entirely unknown in the relevant academic circles.

Membership of the College, whether as member of the staff or as student is not conditional on any specific religious affiliation, and when the College had been established, my own inclination as Principal was to emphasize its relations with the University of London and its autonomy within the framework of the University rather than its relations with the Catholic Church and the Society of Jesus. I have since thought, however, that my attitude can reasonably be regarded as having been in some respects unrealistic and wrong-headed. 'Unrealistic' in this sense. The College was non-grant-receiving. It did, indeed, receive tuition fees from students who were in receipt of grants from their respective local authorities. But it had agreed not to claim any share in the State grant to the University. It was thus, to a great extent, financially dependent on the English Jesuit Province. The money received in tuition fees was not nearly sufficient to meet the total cost of maintaining the College, and it could not have continued to exist without subsidies from the 'providing body,' namely the English Jesuit Province. To think in terms of autonomy or independence was clearly unrealistic. Further, though by Charter the College was not a specifically Catholic Institution, membership not being conditional on religious affiliation, the University of London had explicitly expressed the hope that the College would make a specifically Roman Catholic contribution to the study of theology in the University, and the College was glad to fill a particular gap in what might be described as the ecumenical spectrum. I was not, of course, hoping to convert the college into a purely secular institution. That would have been absurd. Looking back, however, I can quite understand that in the eyes of some colleagues I showed insufficient appreciation of the particular religious heritage of the College and of its task of making a specifically Roman Catholic contribution to the study of theology within the University. Juridically, as I have explained, it was a new College, created by Royal Charter. At the same time it is really not surprising if some colleagues laid a heavier emphasis than I did on the element of continuity with the old

Heythrop. It is possible that to some colleagues my attitude was too much what might be expected from a philosopher.

Anyway, what with one thing and another I found my life as Principal as not being in all respects a bed of roses, and I not unnaturally thought it desirable, even imperative, to 'get away from it all' now and then. I am rather hazy about precise dates, but I think that it was in the summer of 1971 that for some three weeks I took the place of the parish priest of Ochtendung, while he had his annual holiday. Ochtendung is a small town between Koblenz and the Eiffel. The population was predominantly Catholic, and there was an excellent attendance at the Sunday Masses. Congregations must have found my German rather trying, but their singing had the firm loud resonance which one associates with Germany, and I found it a joy to listen to. I was well looked after by the parish priest's sister, who kept house for him and took her holiday after his return. She had two small children staying with her, a nephew and niece, and we all enjoyed some expeditions together. There were also several families who showed me kind hospitality, and my visit constituted a refreshing change from life at Heythrop.

It was, I think, in the summer vacation of 1972 and 1974 that I was able to join package-tours to different areas of the Soviet Union. I had been interested in Russia and Russian literature from my schoolboy years, but I had never been to the country before my first package-tour. Besides such obvious centres as Leningrad, Moscow and Kiev, this tour also took one to Tashkent, Khiva, Samarkand, Bukhara and Dushanbe. It was certainly tiring, but, in my opinion, well worth it. The second tour, in 1974, included cities in Azerbaijan, Armenia and Georgia. The time spent in the south was all too short. In particular I should have liked to have been able to see more of the mountains and lakes of Georgia. Incidentally, it was at the close of this second tour that I acted for some hours as an unpaid Intourist guide.

The situation was this. We had flown from Tbilisi in Georgia to Leningrad and were due to return to London by a certain plane on the next Sunday morning. On arrival at Leningrad, however, the tour-guide apologetically informed us that the plane in question no longer operated and that we should have to take a plane bound for London on the Saturday evening. This did not really matter to me personally, as I was resident in London and had my key to Heythrop College. But some of my fellow tourists, from various parts of England, had made special arrangements for being met on the Sunday. They were naturally upset and proceeded to expostulate and kick up a fuss. So the next morning the guide got in touch with Moscow, and as a result we were told that we could fly to Moscow on the Saturday evening, spend the night in a hotel and take a plane in the morning which would get us to London at more or less the same time as we should have arrived according to previous plans. So far, so good. But after dinner on the Saturday the guide announced that she had finished her job and that as she lived in Leningrad, she was not accompanying us to Moscow. Instead, she handed me a pile of passports and told me that it was up to me to get the party into the Hotel Rossia in Moscow and out to the airport in the morning in good time for the plane to London. In the end we got to bed in the Hotel Rossia about 1:00 a.m. To my great relief all the members of the party were ready with their luggage at 6:30 a.m. to board the bus, which turned up after some delay. I doubt, however, whether we would have all boarded the plane in time, had it not been for a young Australian and his vigorous girlfriend who, having succeeded in getting their money changed, undertook to see to the registration of the baggage, while I was trying to persuade two elderly ladies that if they had lost their receipts for the cashing of travellers cheques there was little point in holding up our boarding of the plane while they tried to get the relevant official to accept their word that they had changed so much sterling into roubles, that they had actually spent only part of the sum, and that therefore they should be repaid in sterling what they had not spent. For the official would have to be able to produce the receipts on demand.

I had already suspected that talk about our original plane no longer operating was bogus, and that the authorities had overbooked or given our seats to a more important group of people, ballet-dancers or trade-unionists or something of the sort. And in fact, when we arrived at London, we encountered some other tourists who had just arrived from Leningrad by the plane which was said to be no longer operating. Of course, these were the days before the proclamation of *Glasnost*.

As far as I was concerned, these two tours were very satisfactory, and I think that my fellow-tourists were also satisfied. The guides were almost always friendly, pleasant and patient, and we were well fed by Intourist. Some elderly ladies complained, rather to my annoyance, that we were given too much to eat. I saw no good reason to discourage Intourist in its culinary arrangements. Further, Intourist was scrupulous in seeing that we had the meals for which we had paid in advance. This was so much the case that one day, when plane delays had meant that we missed lunch at the accustomed time, we were offered lunch on arriving at our destination at about five or six in the afternoon, a copious dinner being promised for about nine o'clock. But if I remember correctly, some of the party objected to consuming two heavy meals one after the other, and the promised dinner was converted into something rather lighter, with wine on the house, while we watched some dancing. This was appreciated by all concerned.

Needless to say, people join package-tours in the Soviet Union in order to see things rather than to eat. And even if I did not see all that I would have liked to have seen, I certainly saw the sort of things which I wanted to see. It used frequently to be said, 'they will show you only what they want you to see.' This warning left me cold. I had no wish to see factories, military installations or labour camps. What I wanted to see was scenery, museums, churches, palaces, ancient mosques, and these are the sort of things which I did see. Are we in England ac-

customed to say to groups of foreign tourists, "No, we are
not going to the Tower of London or Westminster Abbey
or the British Museum; we shall be spending an interesting morning in going round a factory for manufacturing
collar studs, and in the afternoon we are going to pass a
couple of happy hours in Wormwood Scrubbs gaol?"

The fact that I was just an ordinary tourist did not
exempt me from one or two odd experiences. On my first
tour I was in my room in a Moscow hotel when I received
a mysterious telephone call one day. "Are you listening?"
"Yes, I am listening, but I don't really understand what
you are saying." Whether it was a case of a mistaken
number or whether someone wished to propose an illegal
transaction or whether the speaker wished to ascertain
whether I spoke fluent Russian, I do not know. On my
second tour, however, I received a call which was rather
less ambiguous. I was in my hotel room in Tbilisi, when a
woman rang me and started talking in Russian. As far
as I could make out, she wanted to meet me. She certainly asked what floor I was on in the hotel. When I
asked whether I knew her, she laughed merrily and said
'No.' Apparently this was a situation which could be easily remedied. I tried to explain that though I could produce a Russian phrase or two, I could not understand
Russians speaking, and certainly not if they spoke at the
normal rate. The woman simply laughed and went on
talking. In the end I said that I was sorry but I could
not really follow what she was saying. With that I rang
off. Presumably no Russian lady would have rung up a
foreigner in an Intourist hotel without the connivance,
knowledge or direction of the KGB. But there was no
use, of course, in attempting to get a true explanation out
of our guide.

One evening in Tbilisi I went for a walk along the
main boulevard, and, feeling tired, I sat down on a bench.
At that time I still smoked, and I rolled and lit a ciga-
rette. Presently an elderly couple sat down on the same
bench, and the gentleman engaged me in conversation.
On learning that I was English, he remarked that he
spoke little English but that he and his wife both spoke

French. So I did my best to carry on in my execrable French. After a while the man asked whether I would care to accompany him and his wife to a large park where we could talk more freely. When I ascertained that the park was some distance off, I excused myself and said that I was expected back to supper with my tourist group. The man remarked that I could have supper with his wife and himself. But he did not press me, and after courteous old-world farewells we parted. Perhaps he wanted to tell me his life story, and it is possible that by going with him, as invited, I might have learned much of interest. But in the Soviet Union things were not always what they seemed to be, and I opted in favour of prudence. How was I to know that I would not be the unintending means of getting the pair into trouble?

I am not a lover of congresses, international or otherwise; but in the summer of 1973 I went to the international philosophical congress in Varna. The Committee of the Congress kindly gave me hospitality while the congress was in session, and the British Academy did me the honour of nominating me as one of its representatives (together with Sir Alfred Ayer) and gave me a grant to cover the travel expenses. I was therefore glad to take the opportunity of visiting Bulgaria, even at the cost of listening to a lot of talk which I did not really wish to hear.

When I arrived by plane at Sofia, I looked round to see whether there was anyone from Balkantourist to meet me, but in the crush it looked as though making contact might cause some difficulty. While, however, I was standing in the queue at the controls, I suddenly heard someone saying in English "There is Mr. Copleston." I looked up and saw a man, whom I assumed to be an American, pointing me out to a guide. "Thank you," I said. "I wondered what I was going to do. As you know who I am, I assume that you are a fellow philosopher, who is also on his way to the congress." "I know who you are," the man replied with a smile, "but I am not a philosopher." No further explanation was vouchsafed of how he was able to recognize me.

Some days later, when I was taking a few days' holiday at Borovets before going on to Varna, I was walking back through the woods to my hotel, when I heard the same voice saying, "And here is Mr. Copleston once again." He was walking up the path with two companions. We passed the time of day, and my benefactor of the airport said: "You told me that you were going to a congress." "Yes, I replied, but the congress does not start until the twenty-sixth (or whatever), and meanwhile I am having a few days holiday in the mountains." The man then asked if the path led to the ski lift. "Yes, it does, but the machine stops working in about half an hour. If you go up the mountain now, you will probably have to find your way down in the dusk." "That doesn't matter," said the man, "we are out from the city for some fresh air." The mountain was not, as far as I knew, a dangerous one, but I thought it most unlikely that the three men, dressed, as they were, in city clothes and shoes, seriously intended to go up the mountain in the ski lift at that late hour. What intrigued me most, however, was the fact that once again there was no explanation whatsoever of how they came to know who I was or what body they represented. If, as I suppose, they were connected with security or intelligence, they afforded me no assistance in identifying them. They were not unpleasant in any way; they were just mysterious.

When I was back in England, I related the incident to one or two people whom I knew to have been connected with intelligence in the second world war and remarked that I could not understand what interest a foreign security or intelligence service could have in a harmless academic. One of the people to whom I mentioned the incident commented, "Perhaps, Father, you forget to what Society you belong." Another remarked that Bulgarian security people might understandably have wondered what a Jesuit was doing wandering about by himself in the mountains. Obviously, the two comments amounted to much the same thing. When I related to someone else how I had received a mysterious telephone call from some woman when I was staying in a hotel in the Soviet Union, the man said something like this. "The KGB likes to have a large bank of people on whom they can bring pressure, if they think it would be useful. If they had succeeded in compromising you with the help of a woman, you might never have heard any more about it. But if the need arose, they might try to bring pressure on you to do them a service. Obviously, they are well aware that you have no military secrets to impart. But you have a position in academic life, and they might at some time wish to bring pressure on you to find out for them which professor or lecturer in a given college or university suggests possible recruits for one of the British intelligence agencies. Or, if they were suspicious at any time of the intentions of the Jesuit order, they would have someone available whom they could push into obtaining information for them."

I do not recollect that incidents of the kind which I have mentioned ever caused me fear. I was intrigued, and, to tell the truth, I felt rather flattered that any foreign agency would think me worth bothering about. But if one thinks that any such agency is going to satisfy one's curiosity about its intentions and motives, one is obviously mistaken.

At Borovets I was very much on my own. But there were some casual contacts. One evening, when the dining room was very full, owing to an international get-together and an influx of guests, an East German couple, probably recently married and on tour in Bulgaria, sat at my table. We chatted away, and though both were careful what they said, the young lady complained that though there was no great difficulty in their taking a motoring holiday in an eastern block country such as Bulgaria or Romania, visiting the Federal Republic was quite a different matter, in spite of the fact that the inhabitants of both West and East Germany belonged to the same nation. Another afternoon I was sitting on the terrace of the hotel having a cup of coffee, when I was joined by a voluble East German man, perhaps a trades-union boss. While a convinced Communist, he made it clear to me that in his opinion the Germans were the only people who could make Communism work, a task, I gathered, well beyond the capacities of the Russians, let alone the Balkan satellites. I found him a rather entertaining companion while we had our afternoon coffee.

I may seem to have strayed very far from the subject of Heythrop College's move from the Cotswolds to London. Having referred to my felt need, as first Principal of the new College, to 'get away from it all' now and again, I seem to have got bogged down in impressionistic accounts of particular attempts to meet this need. It is time to make a few more remarks relating to Heythrop's life in London, though I have no intention of turning this chapter into a blow-by-blow history of the College's development.

The whole operation, from the opening of discussion of the project of moving to London up to the successful outcome of the formal application to the University, was carried through in a surprisingly short space of time. And the College owes a great debt of gratitude both to the then Principal of the University, Sir Douglas Logan, and other officials of the University, such as the Clerk to the Senate, Dr. L.L. Pownall and the Academic Registrar, Mr. M.A. Baatz, as well as to our friends at King's College, New College and Richmond College. Unfortunately, both New College (first Congregationalist, then United Reformed), and Richmond College (Methodist) found themselves eventually in positions leading them to decide to move elsewhere. The decision was perfectly understandable, but the ecumenical aspect of the study of theology in the University was thereby impoverished.

As was mentioned above, Heythrop College in Oxfordshire was at first an institution in which young Jesuits pursued their ecclesiastical studies, philosophical and theological, the teaching being done by Jesuit lecturers. When Heythrop became a Pontifical Athenaeum, the student body (and the staff) became considerably more varied. At the same time the great majority of the students looked forward to ordination either as priests belonging to some religious order or as diocesan priests. In other words, the great bulk of the students can be described as pursuing studies with a view to ordination as Catholic priests, whether religious (belonging to a religious order) or diocesan. In London, however, we began to receive students who wished to study for a theological degree or diploma of the University of London with a view not to ordination but, most probably, to teaching religion (to use an odd and somewhat objectionable phrase) in secondary schools. Nowadays teachers can hardly get by on the basis of some Christian piety alone. A lot more is required to cope with the needs of boys and girls today.

Since we first went to London, the number of such students, sometimes described as 'lay' in distinction from 'clerical' or 'ordination students' has tended to increase. This is, of course, an excellent development. But it is also an excellent thing that some at any rate of those students who are looking forward to ordination should have the opportunity of pursuing their studies preparatory to the priesthood not in an isolated seminary but in a constituent College of a great University. Before the move to London some timorous souls expressed fears that studying philosophy and theology in a secular university would result in students losing their faith or at least in abandonment by clerical students of their status. But things have not worked out in this way.

In June 1970 a Committee of Enquiry into the Governance of the University of London was appointed, under the chairmanship of Lord Murray of Newhaven, by the University and the University Grants Committee. At the time when the Committee invited Schools of the University and interested persons to submit evidence, Heythrop had not yet received its Royal Charter and been admitted as a School of the University of London. None the less the Committee kindly invited the College to submit evidence, and I found myself exchanging formal letters with my brother who had recently retired from his position as Secretary of the University Grants Committee and had accepted the temporary post of Secretary to Lord Murray's Committee. On December 8, 1970, seven or eight members of the Committee, including the Chairman and Secretary, visited Heythrop and talked with representatives of the administration, the academic staff and the student body. The final report of the Committee appeared in the autumn of 1972. It contained recommendations in regard to the future of the Theological Schools of the University which were certain to meet with a mixed reception in these institutions. As I had my own opinions about the issues raised and foresaw that they might be somewhat different from the views of the College as a whole, I submitted a personal memorandum, as an individual professor, to the Consultative Committee set up by the Court and Senate of the University to consider the recommendations of the Murray Report. Later on, under another hat, I had the task of drafting a memorandum for the Academic Board of the College to submit to the Academic Council of the University. I drafted it, of course, according to what seemed to be the general consensus of opinion, and with some amendments it was accepted by the Board and duly forwarded to the Academic Council. This memorandum was also incorporated in the memorandum which was eventually submitted by the College as a whole in the name of the Governing Body. (Some ideas of my own, for which the College was not, of course, responsible, were expressed in an informal manner in an article included in the issue of the University Bulletin for January 1974).

It was a condition of my appointment as a professor of the University that I should retire from my chair at the end of the academic session in which I reached the age of 67. This meant, in effect, that I would retire on the 30th of September, 1974. This did not necessarily involve retirement from the office of Principal, which was a matter for the Governing Body of the College itself, not for the University. Having reason, however, to believe that the Governing Body would probably fix the normal age for the Principal's retirement at 67, I thought it only proper to submit to the Governors my resignation as Principal from the same date as my retirement from my chair. I therefore sent a formal letter of resignation in the summer of 1973, thus giving the Governing Body plenty of time to select a successor. It had, indeed, been generally assumed that the first Principal would or might remain in office until the end of the College's five-year probationary period and, as we hoped, its permanent recognition as a School of the University. When, however, the Chairman of the Governing Body asked me to inform him of my personal wishes before my letter of resignation was put before the Governors, I made it clear that I should prefer not to be invited to continue as Principal for another period.

There is, of course, nothing odd in a man of my age resigning from an administrative post. In the Civil Service the age of retirement was considerably lower. Moreover, the spectacle of someone clinging to office when he or she should make way for a younger person is not a pleasing one. If for some good reason my fellow Governors had thought it necessary to press me to stay on for a while in spite of my declared wish to resign, I would have been prepared to accept their decision. But as they decided to respect my wish, there is no more to be said. At the same time I would not like it to be thought that I expressed a wish that my resignation should be accepted simply because I wanted more time to write or to go to the United States or something of the sort. I did, indeed, hope to have more time for writing, but this was certainly not my main motive, especially as I doubted whether at my age I should be able to write anything of much value. The fact of the matter was that I saw, or thought that I saw, a considerable difference of opinion emerging between a good many members of the staff and myself in regard to the desirable development of the College. I do not claim that my ideas were the correct ones. The point is that I came to the conclusion that if the academic staff of the College was set on pursuing a policy with which, at that time at any rate, I was not really in sympathy, it was desirable that I should be succeeded by someone who would promote the policy in question more wholeheartedly than I felt inclined to do. I was, of course, quite capable of recognizing that there would be no point in the Society of Jesus maintaining at very considerable expense another 'neutral' College in the University of London. At the same time I found myself in agreement with some of the recommendations made by the Murray Committee of Enquiry in regard to the development of theological teaching in the University, recommendations which were not regarded with much favour by a number of my colleagues. It may well be the case, however, that at the time I looked on the situation too much from what I took to be the University's point of view and too little from the point of view of a School of the University which desired to preserve its traditions and self-identity. If so, this constituted an excellent reason for a change of Principal. And I have no doubt that this was precisely the conviction of some of my colleagues.

Under my successors the College has developed in such a way as to win respect and a solid reputation for the very creditable academic results obtained by its students. It has survived some serious financial difficulties (being still a non-grant-receiving School of the University), and has consistently performed a valuable task in the field of tertiary education in this country. I regard it as a signal privilege if I was able to play a modest role in contributing to the establishment and initial development of the College.

Chapter 14

Between Retirements

AS RELATED IN THE LAST CHAPTER I RETIRED BOTH AS A professor in the University of London and as Principal of Heythrop College at the end of September 1974. The Senate of the University did me the honour of conferring on me the title of 'Emeritus Professor,' and Heythrop made me an honorary fellow of the College. After leaving the College I took up residence in the Jesuit house attached to Farm Street church, but shortly after Christmas 1974, I went as a visiting professor to the University of Santa Clara in California. During my last year in London I had attended a discussion dinner hosted by Tom Burns, then editor of *The Tablet,* and had got into conversation with a professor from the (postgraduate) law school at Santa Clara, who happened to be spending a sabbatical year in England. In the course of our conversation I mentioned that I would shortly be retiring, and that I had vague ideas of the possibility of doing a spot of teaching in the United States, if any university wished to make use of my services for a while. The professor of law asked me whether he might mention my possible availability to the authorities at Santa Clara. Remembering the attractive campus from a passing visit while on a lecture-tour in the sixties and thinking that California would be just the place for a semester's teaching, I readily agreed. The result was a warm invitation and the beginning of an association which gave me great pleasure.

Santa Clara was originally a small Jesuit foundation, from which it has grown into a university with over seven thousand students. The President is a Jesuit, and there is a significant Jesuit presence, chiefly in the Humanities. But the number of lay teachers, men and women, greatly exceeds the number of Jesuits employed in the university. After all, one would hardly expect to find Jesuits teaching in the school of engineering, and only one or two were employed in the law school. Ultimately, the university is run by the Board of Trustees. For most of the period during which I visited Santa Clara the chairman was Ben Swig, a Jewish millionaire who took a lively interest in education and, though not a Christian, was a generous benefactor and devoted friend of Santa Clara. (The development of the original College into the University of Santa Clara has been admirably recounted by Father Gerald L. McKevitt, S.J. in a work published by the Stanford University Press in 1979.)

Obviously, a problem arises when a religious foundation of one sort or another develops into a modern pluralistic university. A problem arises at any rate if a given university wishes to maintain a continuity with its past which is more than purely historical. At what point, for example, does it become unreasonable to speak of a university as Catholic when there are no religious tests, and members of staff vary from convinced Christians to agnostics? The problem may perhaps seem to be a purely linguistic one, in the sense that it is a question of when the application of a certain label, once apt, has become misleading or unreasonable. But it is more than simply a question of words. It certainly happens that parents encourage their sons and daughters to apply for entrance to a university such as Santa Clara because they believe that it is in some real sense a Catholic institution. Labels apart, at what point would it become unreasonable to claim that their expectations are fulfilled? If, for instance, in a given university there is a religious studies department, and if in this department no presuppositions are made about the truth (or falsity) of Christianity or of any other religion, how does this situation affect the issue?

Santa Clara has shown itself acutely aware of this kind of problem and the relevant issues have been much discussed. It is true, I think, that at Santa Clara, as at other universities which find themselves in similar or analogous situations, everyday life proceeds smoothly enough without the relevant problems constantly intruding themselves and demanding attention. But when an originally homogeneous college develops into a pluralist university, it is not surprising if complaints are heard from parents and former students that the place is no longer what it was and has become or is in process of becoming thoroughly secularized.

As far as Santa Clara was concerned, I did not think that the university could do much more than it was already doing to preserve continuity with its past, not at any rate without impairing its status and reputation as an excellent modern 'private' university. However, having drawn attention to the problem, I proceed to leave it aside. It is by no means peculiar to Santa Clara, of course.

Happily, I was not expected to shoulder the heavy classload customary in American universities. During the period when I was a visiting professor at Santa Clara, I was there for two terms each academic year. At first I gave either two classes a term (with four weekly lectures in each course) or one lecture-course and one seminar. Later on my teaching-load was reduced. I also gave some public lectures at Santa Clara and elsewhere. As for my experience of American students as compared with those in Britain, it seemed to me that in regard to degrees of mental ability one found the same sort of mixture, brilliant, sound, mediocre, poor. At the same time I thought that English undergraduates, on starting their studies, gave evidence of a higher level of preparation at school. In saying this I may be guilty of comparing American students of today with English students of yesterday, but I came across other lecturers who shared my opinion. At the same time there were students at Santa Clara who were as good as one could find anywhere, highly intelligent and interested.

I mentioned above that there was a strong Jesuit presence at Santa Clara. The majority lived together in a house on the campus, and it was here that I stayed during my periods in California. I was given a warm welcome and made to feel thoroughly at home, and I retain the pleasantest memories of life in the Jesuit Community and of the kindness and generosity of my many friends there. It is with particular pleasure that I recall week ends at the villa house which the Community owned in the Santa Cruz mountains or hills. The informal life led there by small groups for a couple of days and the excellent evening meals prepared by cooks among us enabled one to get to know colleagues in a way which was rather less easy back in the university, when we were all busy with our respective classes.

In 1978 the University of Santa Clara did me the honour of conferring on me an honorary doctorate of Humane Letters. I also received honorary doctorates from Creighton University (Omaha), Marquette University (Milwaukee), Rockhurst College (Kansas City) and Loyola University at Chicago.

As I have indicated, in the years in which I went out to the United States as a visiting professor, I usually spent two terms of the academic year at Santa Clara. The exception was the year when I went as a visiting professor in the department of philosophy to the University of Hawaii at Honolulu during the second semester of the academic year, 1975-76, that is to say from January to May 1976. As this is a State university, I had to take a notarized oath at the American embassy in London, before going to Hawaii, that I would not conspire to subvert the government of the United States. Having no intention of attempting anything of the kind, I had no hesitation in taking the oath and becoming, I suppose, a temporary civil servant.

At the university I gave a course on modern philosophy from Descartes onwards to a large class of undergraduates and conducted a seminar on Hegel for graduate students. A lot of good work was done in the department of philosophy, but one could hardly claim that the climate of Hawaii encourages feverish activity, and the splendid beaches, with the warm water in the lagoons, constituted an abiding temptation, for me, of course, as well as for others. I liked my students and was glad to see any who wished to visit me outside class (otherwise they went to my teaching assistant with their queries), but it would have been unreasonable to expect from them more than a fairly modest degree of application to philosophical study.

The department of philosophy was refreshingly pluralistic. The then chairman, Professor D. Kalupahana, came from Sri Lanka and lectured and wrote on Buddhist thought. An Indian professor lectured on Indian philosophy, and Islamic, Chinese and Japanese philosophical traditions were also represented. There were, of course, some western-style analysts, including the logician Professor Copi, and one or two of them at least clearly thought that the proper place for the study of oriental traditions was the department of religious studies, not that of philosophy. Happily, however, the pluralists were holding their own. After all, Hawaii is a meeting-place of East and West, with an ethnically mixed population, and it is only proper that a variety of philosophical traditions should be studied in the department of philosophy. I do not know how the situation has developed since the time of my sojourn in Hawaii, but I very much hope that the department has not succumbed to pressure exercised by those who adhere to a rather narrow idea of philosophy.

In my capacity as a visiting professor, I was concerned with western philosophy, but my duties were not really exacting, and I was able to use the opportunities offered and give some time to the study of eastern thought, so far as one who is ignorant of the relevant oriental languages was able to do this. Needless to say, I was able to use the university library, and Professor Eliot Deutsch, a specialist in the Advaita tradition of Hindu thought, was so kind as to loan me books from his extensive private library. The results of my amateur stud-

184 / *Memoirs of a Philosopher*

ies eventually bore modest fruit in my *Philosophies and Cultures* and in the text of my Gifford lectures, *Religion and the One*. (In the meantime I had supplemented my reading by making use of the oriental library at Oxford.)

Before leaving England I had met Professor John Passmore, of the Australian National University at Canberra, at the house of Professor Sir Alfred Ayer. In the course of conversation I mentioned that I was soon going to Hawaii as a visiting professor, and Passmore suggested that afterwards I should go on to Australia. He would obtain for me a position as a Visiting Fellow in the research part of the university at Canberra. When, therefore, the semester at Honolulu had come to an end, I flew to New Zealand, where I gave some lectures at Christchurch and elsewhere, and then went on to Australia. The prospect of exchanging the warmth of Hawaii for the Australian winter was somewhat daunting, as I was not equipped for cold weather, but though I developed a bad cold, the weather was not at all so trying as I had feared.

Christchurch in New Zealand seemed to me delightfully old world. Apart, however, from a visit to Mount Cook in the south, I had not much time for sightseeing, though I was rather taken by what I was able to see of the country. When I arrived at Canberra in Australia, I lived with the small and very friendly Jesuit Community, which included Father J. Eddy, who held the post of Reader in the research branch of the National University. At the university I was given an office and a graduate assistant, who tracked down books for me in the library. My duties were far from onerous. I gave, I think, three seminar sessions for staff and graduate students. Otherwise I got on with work of my own. This is, indeed, what was expected of anyone functioning in the research branch of the university. The regular professors in the research branch may supervise graduate students, but they are not called upon to lecture to undergraduates, whose needs are catered for in another branch of the university. In my opinion, this encouragement of research and publication is an admirable feature of the National University. I hope that the arrangement still persists.

After six weeks at Canberra I went to Melbourne, where I gave a number of public lectures and also some talks in the University of Melbourne. At one public lecture, I remember, I was heckled about the doctrine of the Trinity by a professor from a university other than the University of Melbourne. Having made simply a passing reference to the doctrine, I was annoyed by the intervention and refused to be drawn into contoversy on the topic. Looking back, however, I am inclined to think that I ought to have been more forthcoming. If one avoids an issue, one inevitably gives the impression that one has nothing to say in reply to whatever objection or challenge has been raised, even if the topic is not strictly relevant to the subject on which one has just lectured.

Having got as far as New Zealand and Australia in my travels, I was able to return to England by way of the Orient. If I had been some twenty years younger, I dare say that I would have arranged to have broken the return journey to England in a good many places, making use of an opportunity which was unlikely to come my way again. For example, I should like to have been able to touch down at Rangoon and see a little of the city where my father had occupied a judicial post. As it was, I confined my stopovers to Hongkong, Bangkok and Bombay.

The Irish Jesuits in Hongkong could not have been kinder or more helpful, arranging for me to visit two schools and a university. I had no lecture engagements at Hongkong and was simply a tourist. Not having been in the East before, I was fascinated by the teeming life of the city, and I was struck by the great number of young people whom I saw in the streets. At the time of my visit Chairman Mao was still alive, and during an interview with a China-watcher, a Jesuit of Hungarian origin, I remember asking him whether he thought that Madame Mao would take over when her husband died. He replied that in his opinion she was much more likely to get her comeuppance. He turned out to be right.

Though I gave no formal lecture in Bangkok, a professor of the university phoned me and asked whether I would talk informally with some of his students about British philosophy. He said that they would come one afternoon to the Jesuit residence. On the afternoon in question I went into the garden and saw a group of young people sitting in the shade of a tree. I greeted them and started talking about philosophy. After a while someone came out of the house and told me that the students whom I was expecting had arrived. The group of young people whom I was actually addressing must have been rather mystified by my conduct, but they were far too polite to comment on the situation. Having transferred my attention to the right group of boys and girls, I soon realized that neither their knowledge of English nor their philosophical preparation was sufficient to enable them to understand much about contemporary British philosophy. So our conversation became pretty general. I was impressed by both groups as models of politeness, but I am afraid that they did not learn much about British philosophical thought from our encounter.

Needless to say, I visited some of the splendid Buddhist temples and shrines. At a temple in the former Royal compound a guide took it upon himself not only to give some account of Hinyana Buddhism (which was perfectly proper and appropriate, of course) but also to ridicule belief in God, his words being offensive not only to Christians but also to orthodox Jews and Muslims. I could see that a young man in the party, a devout Anglican I think, was put out, but nobody made any comment. The incident surprised me, as it seemed so contrary both to Thai politeness and to the Buddhist spirit. I suspected, however, that the guide might be a Communist of sorts, and that his sympathy with Buddhism did not extend beyond the fact that Hinyana Buddhism does not comprise belief in a personal God.

One afternoon I climbed a steep hill to visit the Buddhist shrine at the top. There seemed to be nobody else about. But when I was removing my shoes to enter the shrine, a young man suddenly appeared, who proceeded to say something to me. At first I was somewhat apprehensive that he might be going to demand money with menaces. But he seemed to be harmless, in spite of his sturdy appearance, and after I had visited the shrine we sat for a while in the sun. He told me that he had been for a period in a Buddhist monastery. When I asked him whether he had enjoyed the experience, he replied with a firm 'no.' It is a very common custom for a Thai man, even a member of the royal family, to spend a short period as a monk, and it may be that the young man had simply conformed to custom. But I think that I remember hearing that sometimes delinquent youths are consigned for a period to a monastery with a view to reformation, and I wondered whether my chance acquaintance had been one of them. But I did not inquire. Anyway, as I had stories of youths in Bangkok accosting foreigners under the pretext of practising their English, luring them into a suitably secluded spot and then demanding their wallets, I was relieved when I safely descended the steep hill and was once more in a street.

At Bombay I talked to the Philosophical Society about philosophical dialogue between East and West. This was doubtless a suitable topic, but one is faced by the difficulty that, for all one knows, one's hearers have studied in the West and have adopted western lines of thought, looking on their native philosophical traditions in a light analogous to that in which many western philosophers regard the thought of the Middle Ages. Discussion after my lecture suggested that the classical Indian philosophical traditions were primarily of historical interest and had little relevance today.

I was also taken to a Technical University to give a talk to an audience of students. I forget what I talked about, but after the talk the Director, the Assistant Director and a group of staff entertained me to tea. In the course of the conversation it became clear to me that some at least of my hosts were Marxists who had studied (engineering, for example) at Moscow. Most were polite and friendly enough, but one man showed some hostility and asserted roundly that religion had been the curse of

India and that India did not need any more, whether imported or native. He obviously thought of religion as fostering escapism and a purely inward-looking attitude, whereas what India needed was dynamic socially-oriented attitudes. I tried to make some relevant remarks, but the gentleman's rather evident hostility hardly encouraged dialogue.

After a few years at the Jesuit residence in Mount Street I was transferred to Campion Hall, Oxford, where I had my base for some eight years. In 1975 I had been elected an Honorary Fellow of my old College, St. John's, and I greatly treasured the association with the College which residence in Oxford made possible. On Sundays in term time, for example, I generally attended Evensong in the College chapel and dined afterwards at High Table. The election caused me some surprise, as I had not distinguished myself in any way during my undergraduate days. But I dare say that I was thought to have 'made good' in subsequent years. Anyway, the honour done me gave me a great deal of pleasure.

In the Michaelmas Term of my first year at Oxford I gave the initial series of annual lectures at Campion Hall in memory of Father Martin D'arcy, who had been a distinguished Master of the Hall. The text of the lectures was subsequently published by the Oxford University Press under the title *Philosophers and Cultures*. Then during the autumns of 1979 and 1980 I gave a series (more exactly two series) of Gifford lectures at Aberdeen, the text of which was published by Search Press as *Religion and the One. Philosophies East and West*. In both years I lived on the university campus while giving the lectures and thus was able to get to know members of staff in the Divinity and Philosophy departments. Apart from the actual lectures, given at the rate of one a week, I took over a few classes for the professor of ecclesiastical history, speaking about medieval thought, and gave a seminar session on Hegel for staff and graduate students in the department of philosophy. My stay in Aberdeen was made very pleasant by Scottish hospitality, and I made a number of friends. I was also glad of the opportunity to learn something more about the Church of Scotland from members of the department of Divinity. On Sundays I sometimes attended the morning service in the university church, entering with the academic procession.

In the summer of 1981, after I had finished my work at Santa Clara, I spent three months in the University of Calgary in Alberta, Canada, first as a visiting professor in the summer session and then as a Visiting Scholar in the Humanities Institute. In the first capacity I conducted a seminar on medieval philosophy jointly with Professor A. Parel, the then chairman of the department of political science. In the second capacity I gave some public lectures sponsored by Dr. H.G. Coward, director of the Calgary Institute for the Humanities, but I had plenty of time to get on with preparing a history of philosophy in Russia, on which I was engaged at the time and which was published in Britain and the United States in 1986.

My teaching-load at Santa Clara had been progressively reduced, and I began to think that I was exploiting the generosity of the university, and that it was about time that I staged a second retirement. It is true that the university made no such suggestion, but I felt that at a somewhat advanced age I had better abandon any regular teaching, settle down in Oxford and devote my remaining energies to writing. Besides, health problems were beginning to arise. So with great regret I pulled out in the summer of 1982, at the close of the academic year.

In June 1983 the University of Uppsala conferred on me an honorary doctorate of theology. Though I can hardly claim to be much of a theologian, I greatly appreciated this honour from Sweden's oldest university. As for the elaborate ceremonies, I am not likely to forget them. On the day preceding the conferment of the degree I attended a lunch arranged by the Faculty of Theology, delivered a public lecture on problems in a moral philosophy arising out of Russian thought, went to a subsequent reception, and then went to another reception, this time

given by the Rector Magnificus of the university, which
was followed by a rehearsal for the conferment ceremony.
Next day's proceedings started with salvoes of artillery at
7:00 a.m., while at 8:00 the cathedral bells took up the
good work. The actual conferment ceremony began at
midday and lasted about three hours. As each candidate
came forward to receive the insignia of the relevant honorary doctorate, a detachment of the Swedish army fired
a salvo and an orchestra discoursed sweet music. The
conductor of the orchestra could, of course, see what was
going on, but as the army detachment was stationed outside, there must have been an efficient system of communication. The other recipient of an honorary doctorate in
theology was a Finnish Lutheran bishop, a former university professor, but there were a good many other recipi-
ents of honorary doctorates, from various countries. As
for ordinary doctors, so to speak, I was amused to hear
them addressed as *carissimi iuvenes*, in spite of the fact
that some of them hardly looked young.

After the ceremony the Lutheran Primate of Sweden,
the Archbishop of Uppsala, very kindly invited me and a
few other people to drink some champagne in his mansion. He and his wife were very gracious, and I was glad
to meet them. After this interlude I returned to the
small Jesuit residence, where I was staying, to change
into dress clothes (hired by me in Uppsala) for the banquet in the castle. The actual meal, at which there were
seven speeches and some singing by a choir, lasted over
three hours. When, however, people adjourned for coffee,
further potation and dancing, I retrieved my top hat (part
of the doctorate insignia) and departed, having previously
ascertained that this would not be looked on as unacceptable behaviour. By the time dinner was over I felt quite
exhausted, especially as I was not used to the 'white
nights' of June and had found it somewhat difficult to get
to sleep.

The visit to Uppsala was not the only foreign trip
which I made in the course of 1983. In November I spent
some three weeks in Japan, at the invitation of Sophia
University in Tokyo. Besides giving some lectures at So-

phia and at one or two other centres in the capital, such as Keio University, I also lectured at Nagoya and Kyoto. At Nagoya I stayed with the Fathers of the Divine Word. In the mornings I concelebrated with the priests, and I was interested to find a young Japanese Buddhist sitting with us. Not being a Christian, he did not communicate, but he liked to be present at what was really an intimate Christian meeting of just a few people. A brief visit to Japan obviously does not qualify me to pontificate about its inhabitants and their ways, but I received the distinct impression that those Japanese who took religion in any way seriously were much given to a tolerant openness to most of the religions which had a foothole in Japan. For example, one might be married by Shinto priests and buried by Buddhist monks. It seemed, moreover, to be becoming quite fashionable to get married in a Christian church. In other words, Japanese happily combined Shintoism and Buddhism, and it seemed to me that they would also be happy to include Christianity if Christians did not demand an exclusive allegiance. A westerner, of course, is inclined to object that one can hardly believe all the tenets of Shintoism, Buddhism and Christianity at the same time, but I very much doubt whether belief in the sense in which a westerner would be likely to understand the term generally occupies a prominent position, or even any position, in the Japanese religious outlook. When I was at Nagoya I was taken to visit the impressive Shinto shrine of Ise with its wonderful natural setting, and I could quite understand that to ask whether Japanese visitors to the shrine really believed in the Shinto myths was to ask a question which was in an important sense irrelevant, even if for a westerner it was a natural question to raise. Visiting the shrine and communing with nature were presumably accompanied by some sort of experience or experiences which certainly could not be properly described as endorsing the truth of certain propositions. Presumably the young Buddhist to whom I referred above found that being present at a Christian concelebrated Mass in an intimate and friendly setting provided him with an experience which he valued and found genuinely helpful, without committing himself either to endorsing or denying the truth of the relevant Christian beliefs. To be sure, as far as this particular young man is concerned, my interpretation of his attitude may be wide of the mark. But it does, I think, reflect an attitude which is common enough among Japanese who are open to the influence of religion.

In Kyoto I had the good fortune to be taken round some of the famous Buddhist temples by Father K. Kadowaki, S.J., author of a book entitled *Zen and the Bible*. He had been an adherent of Zen Buddhism before his conversion to Christianity, and he remained convinced that Zen Buddhism contains elements of real value. We were accompainied for much of our temple-tour by a Japanese university student, Osamu Nakamura, but in the evening I was alone with Father Kadowaki, and when we visited the sand-and-rock garden of the Ryoanji temple, which was then deserted (as Father Kadowaki had obtained permission for us to stop on when other visitors had left), my companion seemed to have become immersed in Zen meditation, and as I was flying to England the next day and therefore wanted to catch the 'bullet train' back to Tokyo that evening, I began to get apprehensive. However, all went well.

During the time that I spent in Tokyo the presence of Father Peter Milward, S.J. and Father Michael Cooper, S.J. at Sophia University was a great help. I had known both of them in England, before they devoted themselves to work in Japan, and if in my short time in Japan I came to learn anything at all of Japanese ways and attitudes, it was mainly due to them.

It may seem that in the course of my life I have done a lot of travelling in foreign countries. Well, I have, of course, done a good deal. But there were also plenty of other invitations which, for one reason or another, I did not accept. And now I have lost all inclination to leave my own country. As a velleity I may from time to time regret that I have not been here or there or seen this or that or that I cannot recapture an experience which I once enjoyed, but I know very well that I am no longer prepared to undertake anything but short and easy journeys in my own land. Nor am I any longer prepared to cope with the effort to speak a foreign language. In other words, advancing age tells in the end.

Chapter 15

Changes in the Church

IT WOULD BE NATURAL FOR ANY READER OF THE CHAPTER of these memoirs in which I tried to indicate the reasons for my seeking reception, when I was still a schoolboy, into the Catholic Church, to wonder how my newly found religious allegiance has worn with the years. For example, I became a Catholic with the confidence that the Church which I was joining was and would remain a firm and unchanging rock in a sea of change. How have I reacted to the changes in the life of the Church which were heralded by Pope John XXIII's call to *aggiornamento* and by the second Vatican Council which he convened? Have I perhaps lived to regret my abandonment of the Anglican Church, especially when, as I have openly stated, this caused great distress to my father? Again, given the years which I have spent in studying and writing about the historical development of philosophical thought in, for the most part, the West, and given the friendly relations which it has been my good fortune to enjoy with some philosophers who were far from sharing my religious convictions, to what extent, in my estimation have these factors affected my religious beliefs? Have I perhaps found philosophical reflection threatening to corrode or to undermine not simply my confidence in the claims of the Catholic Church as distinct from other Christian bodies but also in the truth (possibly even the meaningfulness) of basic Christian beliefs? If so, how have I tried to cope with the situation? Have I been driven to abandon either philosophy on the one hand or Christian faith on the other? Or have I tried to overcome any tensions which have arisen between them in my mind? If so, have I reached any sort of solution which seems to me satisfactory?

It should be obvious that in the final chapter of an autobiography I cannot be reasonably expected to provide a theological-philosophical treatise. But the sort of questions mentioned above are natural ones to ask, and I feel that if these memoirs have any readers, the latter would be justified in feeling let down, were I to pass over the relevant topics in unbroken silence.

As for immediately noticeable changes such as the introduction and progressive spread, since the second Vatican Council, of the use of the vernacular in the sacred liturgy (of the Latin Church) they have not caused me any distress, when, that is to say, they have been approved by the relevant authority. It is perfectly understandable, of course, that people may well treasure what they have been accustomed to from early years and resent any change. My old friend, Lady Boynton, to whom I referred in chapter twelve, detested the use of English in the Mass, and she amused me by exclaiming, if I happened to say something in favour of the change, 'But God understands Latin.' It is all very well to talk about preserving an air of mystery and reverence. But while there is obviously something in this line of thought, it seems clear to me that the Mass should be seen as the common worship of the Christian community, priest and people together, and not as a kind of magical rite performed by priests speaking inaudibly, while each member of the congregation gets on with his or her private devotions.

What about the Catholic Church's participation in the ecumenical movement? At the time when I was received into it, actual participation in religious services of a religious body, Christian or otherwise, not in communion with Rome, was strictly forbidden. All that was permitted was physical presence, to avoid giving offence or when common politeness demanded it, at, for example, weddings or funerals, or if a person held an official position which demanded his or her presence at a religious ceremony, as in the case of a Catholic Earl-Marshal at the sovereign's coronation in Westminster Abbey. Then one fine day what had been strictly forbidden was permitted; what had been discouraged was encouraged. How has this remarkable change affected me?

To answer this question I must make a distinction. If we are considering the ecumenical movement in itself, I am very much in favour of it. It is true that I cannot claim to have contributed much, if anything, to furthering ecumenical relations, certainly not if this is understood as preaching frequently in the churches or chapels of other Christian denominations, sitting on a lot of committees, and going to joint-services at frequent intervals. But this is not due to any disapproval of ecumenism, on the ground, for example, that it encourages religious indifferentism. For good or for evil, my energies have been chiefly expended on lecturing and writing on philosophical topics. And though it may be shocking for an octogenarian to have to admit, I have no great enthusiasm nowadays for occupying pulpits or for participating in services, whether joint or otherwise. But I am certainly not upset by efforts to promote closer relations between Christians belonging to different denominations. I certainly do not look on such developments as constituting a betrayal of the past. In so far as they negate the past, the past may very well be something which it was high time to negate. I have already related how after my reception into the Catholic Church the then Bishop of Clifton told me that though I was entitled to put in an appearance at family prayers if absence would cause notable offence, I ought not to join in, even in the recitation of the Our Father, as this would be an act prohibited by the Church. It is hardly a matter for regret if this policy has been left behind.

As for relations between the Catholic Church and non-Christian religions, one should not close one's eyes to the danger of abandoning Christian belief in the unique status and role of Christ and treating him simply as one among other prophets and religious leaders, a danger which is by no means illusory. At the same time Christians should certainly be prepared to recognize the values present in other religions. Short of embracing all mankind there can be no limit to the reach of the out-going love which lies at the heart of the Christian religion, and which can be seen as demanding the extension of the ecumenical movement to relations between Christians and adherents of other religions.

Though, however, changes such as the spread of the vernacular in the sacred liturgy and active participation by the Catholic Church in the ecumenical movement seem to me to constitute changes for the better, changes to be welcomed, the process of change may give rise to some cynical thoughts. This, I admit, has sometimes happened in my own mind, when, for example, I have reflected how the authorities of the Church once insisted that avoidance of participation in non-Catholic worship was willed by God and then at a later date encouraged what they had previously condemned, once more in the name of God.

A natural comment on this line of thought is that it makes no allowance for the fact of historical change. It is not, for example, as though the Church first claimed that God ordered the use of Latin in the liturgy and that on some later day he permitted use of the vernacular. Considered in itself, either line of conduct lay open to the Church. The use of a uniform language in the so-called 'Latin Church' is historically explicable, and the later introduction of the vernacular is also understandable in the light of historical circumstances. The Church came to see a greater use of the vernacular in religious rites as part of what was required by the process of *aggiornamento*, of modernization or updating, the need for which was recognized and proclaimed by Pope John XXIII.

To be sure, in western Christendom, when attacks were made from the Protestant side on the use of a dead language in the liturgy, reasons were advanced by Catholic writers in defence of the continued use of Latin in the

Catholic Church. But it was perfectly well known, of course, that in the eastern Churches Latin was not employed, and, as far as I am aware, it was never seriously maintained by Catholic ecclesiastical authority that the use of a particular language was enjoined by divine revelation. However much in the past the Church authorities may have disapproved of Catholics who insisted on questioning a longstanding practice, such questioning was not, in itself, deemed to be heresy. But what, it may be asked, do I think of the call of some theologians for the restatement of basic Christian doctrines, on the ground that the traditional formulations have become increasingly opaque or misleading, perhaps even unintelligible? Do I regard this sort of programme as commendable, or do I look on it as threatening the concept of revealed truth and as forming a kind of Trojan horse in the City of God?

Let us assume that the concept of restatement in the present context is understood as referring to the attempt to make doctrines such as the Incarnation and the real presence of Christ in the Blessed Sacrament more easily understandable by the ordinary Catholics who have had little or no theological training, with special attention to the attempt to illustrate and bring home the relevance of such doctrines to practice, to the living of a Christian life. There can hardly be any cogent objection to this sort of programme. It has always been seen as a basic task of preachers to do their best to cultivate in the minds of the faithful a better understanding of Christian doctrine, especially with a view to deepening and intensifying the leading of a Christian life.

Those theologians, however, who have espoused the cause of doctrinal restatement are apt to take a dim view of the suggestion that their proper job is one of popularization, of finding, for example, arresting images or pictures intended to convey to the unsophisticated man or woman in the pew a clearer grasp of some doctrine which may hitherto have appeared to him or her as baffling and the relevance of which to Christian life is obscure. The professional theologian may very well be prepared to allow that the activity of popularization has an important role to play in the life of the Church. At the same time they claim that the programme with which they personally are concerned is the strictly theological one of restating doctrines of faith in terms of fresh concepts and thought-forms, when traditional formulations have outlived their usefulness and have tended to become hindrances to acceptance. For example, some theologians have inquired whether the doctrine of the real presence of Christ in the Blessed Sacrament could not be restated with the aid of concepts other than that of transsubstantiation. The substance-accident theory has been subjected to much criticism in philosophical circles; and though it is true that the Council of Trent did not intend to canonize, as it were, a particular philosophical theory, continued use of the term 'transsubstantiation' tends to give the impression that the Catholic belief in the real presence is inextricably tied up with a concept which is looked at askance not only by many philosophers but also by many scientists. True, it has been argued that the philosophers and scientists in question misunderstand the term and its implications. But is a process of reconceptualization perhaps possible? Among terms suggested as preferable to 'transsubstantiation' have been 'transfinalization' and 'transsignification.'

The theologians of whom I am thinking do not think of themselves as playing fast and loose with truths of faith. They aim at restating revealed truth, in such a way that the truth is preserved, not distorted, still less abolished or destroyed. It seems clear to me, however, that the concept of transfinalization differs from that of transsubstantiation. Indeed, would not one expect this to be the case, if restatement, as the term is used in the context, is claimed to be the fruit of genuine reconceptualization, and not simply analogous to translation of, for instance, 'young man' into 'jeune homme'? In other words, unless I am thoroughly mistaken about the nature of the activity of restatement, as understood by the theologians of whom I have been thinking, it can come very

close to an attempt to revise and change what has been
taken to be an article of faith.

It is not my intention to assert, either explicitly or
implicitly, that theologians ought not to engage in attempts to rethink Catholic doctrines, when they are
convinced that there is need for this activity. I am not
demanding that their freedom to speculate should be curtailed. But I do find some difficulty in understanding
precisely how the programme of reconceptualization and
restatement should be interpreted. Consider the proposed
restatement of the doctrine of the real presence of Christ
in the Blessed Sacrament in terms of the concept of
transfinalization instead of in terms of transsubstantiation. Would it be correct to think of one and the same
truth being lifted out of one conceptual bed and laid down
in another? If so, what is this truth? It is all very well
to reply that it is the truth of the real presence. If we
are asked what we mean by this, it is difficult to see how
we can avoid employing certain definite concepts or
thought-forms. It can be argued in other words, that we
cannot identify an unconceptualized truth, which, having
been removed from one conceptual bed, is then to be laid
down in another. In this case is there perhaps some difficulty in determing the criteria for deciding whether the
truth which was previously conceptionalized in one form
has been preserved in its subsequent conceptualization?
How can we be sure that the later formulation expresses
the same truth as the earlier formulation, and that the
content has not undergone a change of identity?

We are sometimes told by 'progressives' that we
should think of the Church as seeking the truth, rather
than as being in possession of the truth. That the
Church's theologians seek truth is not a claim which I
would venture or wish to deny. But they discharge this
function as members of the Church, not simply as lone individuals. And the final court of appeal in doctrinal issues can hardly be anything but the Church herself,
speaking as a teaching authority, through what is called
the *magisterium*. To say this, especially if use is made of
the word *magisterium*, may give the impression that one

hankers after the days when any novel-sounding statement or bold idea expressed by a theologian was liable to
prompt speedy censure of some kind from Rome. A policy
of this kind, however, would encourage intellectual stag-
nation and obstruct that development which is a sign of
life. My point is simply that if a theologian claims to be a
Catholic, he or she should act as such operating within
the Church, as one of its members.

We can recall the passage in St. Paul's first epistle
to the Corinthians (chapter 12) in which the apostle
speaks of the Body of Christ, the Christian community, as
possessing different organs, which should work in har-
mony, each performing its own function or functions for
the good of the whole. Whether St. Paul would approve
of one applying what he says in this way may be open to
question. But one might perhaps suggest that while professional theologians should be free to experiment, in the
sense of proposing and discussing doctrinal restatements
when they thought it appropriate, they should be prepared to accept any final decision of the ecclesiastical
magisterium about the disputed acceptability or otherwise
of a given proposed reformulation of doctrine. It is for
the good of the whole that creative thought should enjoy
free play, but it is also for the good of the whole that
unity should not be shattered and lost.

This is all very well, it may be said; but it is of very
little practical use. We are not told, for example, at what
point in an open discussion between theologians, intervention by the *magisterium* becomes justified or appropriate.
Nor are we provided with any clear idea of the form
which such intervention should take, if it does occur.
Presumably, it would take the form of a decision in response to the question whether or not a certain proposed
doctrinal restatement (say 'transfinalization' instead of
'transsubstantiation') was what it was claimed to be. But
a decision of this kind, to be responsible, would surely demand thorough previous consideration by theologians,
whether members of the *magisterium* (in the sense of the
episcopate) or not, or indeed both. But how long should
such consideration be allowed to go on? Till a real con-

202 / Memoirs of a Philosopher

sensus is attained between the interested parties? Till
the question solves itself, so to speak? Or is ecclesiastical authority morally entitled to intervene decisively,
whenever it judges that this is the proper course of action
to pursue? In this case, what becomes of my claim that
freedom in theological discussion should not be stifled?
Edifying references to this or that Scriptural passage
may, indeed, serve to remind one of important ideals,
such as the harmonious working of the organs of the mystical Body of Christ; but, taken by themselves, such references are insufficient to settle practical problems.

This is obviously quite true. On the one hand, real
theological thought cannot flourish and develop without
freedom. On the other hand, the Catholic theologian per-
forms a function in the Church, not outside it. He or she
is called to explore, penetrate and deepen the Church's
understanding of her own faith and its implications. The
task of combining respect for freedom with recognition of
the theologians's mission to act in the service of the
Church, the Christian community, clearly gives rise to
practical problems, which may very well assume different
forms in different historical situations, and also require
somewhat different solutions. One cannot solve all such
problems in advance. But in emphasizing the claims of
one ideal one should endeavour not to forget all others.
This is doubtless a platitude, but it has its applications.

By way of conclusion to this chapter I should like to
refer briefly to a problem which in the modern world has
tended to impress itself increasingly on the minds of
Christians. It is not a problem which originated in
changes effected by the actions of this or that group in
the Catholic Church, such as reforms effected by a Council or by the unusual goings-on of certain Catholic theologians. It can perhaps be said to have been brought
about, or at any rate intensified, by western man's growing knowledge of or acquaintance with societies and cultures of which he previously had, in most cases, only a
vague general idea. It is a problem intensified by a growing knowledge of the world as it is, a knowledge conveyed

by books, papers, magazines, radio and television and increasingly supplemented by travel to foreign lands.

As we are all aware, though the development of our civilization has brought within the bounds of practical possibility conflicts resulting in the destruction of the human race, it has also tended to bring nations and peoples closer together in various ways, making them more interdependent. And it is not at any rate absurd to envisage the possible formation of a world-society by agreement, an heir to the United Nations Organization and characterized by, for example, a unifying technology. The French philosopher Henri Bergson maintained that any such world-society would need a soul; and he believed that this could be derived only from mystical religion, in particular from the Christian religion, conceived as a channel for an influx of active, dynamic love outflowing from God. According to Bergson, Buddhism, for instance, though certainly a religion of universal compassion, fell short of the dynamic qualities of Christian love. In other words, he saw Christianity not as something outmoded and incapable of infusing spiritual life and vigour into modern society but as the most promising agent for fulfilling this need.

This, however, is one of the ideas which is doubted, or even flatly denied, by a great many people. Bergson's line of thought would obviously be questioned not only by atheists and agnostics but also by adherents of a definite religion other than Christianity, Islam for example. What is more, there are doubtless a fair number of people who would claim to be Christians but who feel uneasy with the universalist claims of Christianity and strongly incline to a pluralism, which some would probably commend as more appropriate in these days of ecumenism. Would it not be reasonable, for instance, to regard the Buddha, and not only Jesus, as a Saviour? After all, for many people the Buddha has been and is a Saviour. To confine this role to Jesus seems unduly narrow. It is understandable that at a time when the Jewish people were awaiting a promised Messiah and Saviour of the nation those Jews who were prepared to accept the idea of a suffering Messiah should look to Jesus as sent by God to bring life to his people and to all human beings who turned to him as the one Redeemer. But after all these centuries can the Church's universalist claims be still taken seriously? Does it really take them seriously itself? To put the question succinctly, is it not becoming increasingly difficult to reconcile recognition of Jesus as a man who lived in an area of the Roman Empire many centuries ago with the claims made on his behalf in orthodox, traditional Christianity. Has he not become, as it is sometimes put, 'too small' for the stupendous cosmic role attributed to him by the Church?

This sort of problem exercised the mind of Teilhard de Chardin. As any reader of his works is aware, he thought in terms of the cosmic Christ, of Christ, that is to say, as the centre and goal of creative evolution and of the Christian religion as destined to effect a metamorphosis in the souls of men and women, generating and intensifying a unifying life of love. His thought has been subjected to a good deal of criticism. Some critics, for example, have argued that the connection between Jesus of Nazareth and Teilhard's cosmic Christ is by no means clear. They think of him, in other words, as trying to show that Jesus of Nazareth can reasonably be conceived as Lord and Saviour of the whole of mankind, indeed of the whole world, by making a leap which has little warrant beyond Teilhard's own religious interests. Other critics have emphasized the claim that what Teilhard did was to put together an admixture of scientific ideas, metaphysical speculation and statements of religious faith and then try to pass off the whole thing under the guise of science or as what scientifically based thinking authorizes and supports. Though, however, such lines of criticism cannot simply be dismissed, they may not matter so very much, if we look on Teilhard as attempting to express a general world-view or interpretation of the universe inspired by Christian faith but markedly influenced in its build-up by an idea of evolution, the application of which is admittedly extended well beyond the range of what would normally count as empirical verification. In a sense Teilhard was a visionary, his vision consisting of a Christian world-view. There is, I think, a place for world-views, possible ways of seeing the universe.

Teilhard's world-vision was, from a Christian point of view, markedly optimistic. For him, the whole process of cosmogenesis was moving not only onwards but upwards, towards what he called Omega Point, the point at which he conceived the world as eventually reaching its goal or *telos* in the union of all human beings in the cosmic Christ. The world-process, we might say, is, for Teilhard, the progressive realization of the Good.

While, however, I can and do feel the attraction of a world-vision such as that of Teilhard de Chardin, it seems to me that the objection brought by Gabriel Marcel, namely that the dogma of progress is an 'arbitrary postulate,' and one the compatibility of which with belief in human freedom is questionable, deserves to be taken seriously. It is doubtless true that the orthodox Christian is committed to believing in the ultimate victory of good over evil, but not necessarily in the triumph of the Church within history, in this world. In the eighteenth chapter of St. Luke's gospel Christ is recorded as asking his disciples whether they think that when Christ comes in glory, he will find faith on earth. True, Jesus does not say that no faith will be found on earth, that there will have been a universal apostasy. But what he says hardly reminds us at once of the optimism of Teilhard de Chardin. It brings to mind a rather different picture.

As for myself, I am certainly not prepared to cast a definite vote either in support of Teilhard's vision of the future course of history or to endorse the idea proposed by the Russian philosopher Vladimir Solovyev in his later years, of the coming kingdom of Antichrist, heralding the last days and the final judgment of God. As far as I am concerned, there is more than one possibility. The Christian is not, I think, committed to believing that if Christianity finds itself widely regarded as moribund and as unable to act as an effective source of inspiration, this shows that Christ has failed. Where in the Gospels is he recorded as having assured his followers of a triumphal march through history?

Perhaps I may add that Christ did not claim that if his followers encountered difficulties and opposition they should set to work revising his teaching and adapting it to the spirit of the age. He looked for persevering loyalty. But this does not imply, of course, that all the accretions of centuries should be obstinately held on to and preserved.

Chapter 16

An Old Man's Faith

IF I REMEMBER CORRECTLY, IN A TELEVISION INTERVIEW which took place shortly after his appointment to the see of Westminster, the late Cardinal Heenan was asked whether he had ever been subject to doubts about the truth of his religious beliefs. This may sound an impertinent question for a television interviewer to ask. But Heenan had recently been appointed to the leading episcopal position in the Catholic Church in England and Wales. He was committed to maintaining the truth of a complex of doctrines. And the question whether his religious faith had always been serene and untroubled or whether, as was doubtless the case with many of his listeners, he had ever been disturbed, possibly even tormented by doubt, might reasonably be regarded as a matter of public interest. In the case of an archbishop the question might understandably be considered more relevant than, for example, a query about which football team he supported. Besides, he was not being asked whether he was perhaps a secret unbeliever, but, unless my memory fails me, simply whether he had ever been troubled by doubts, a common enough phenomenon.

Needless to say, I have never occupied anything approaching the eminent ecclesiastical position which Cardinal Heenan came to occupy. But given the facts that I have not only spent many years of my life studying, writing, and talking about the historical development of philosophical thought, that I have paid a good deal of attention to lines of thought which were radically critical of religious belief, and that I have been on friendly relations with a number of agnostics and atheists, it would be natural enough if some observers wondered how my life as a philosopher had affected my life as a religious believer. Have I tried to preserve the two lives entirely separate from one another, each occupying its own watertight compartment? Or have I tried to harmonize them? Or have I, in response to doubt, secretly relinquished one of them in favour of the other? It is true that one would hardly ask such questions of a fellow-guest at a dinner-party; but some reference to such topics might reasonably be expected in a book of memoirs, of a writer who is both a Catholic priest and, in his own small way, a philosopher. To be sure, there are some other philosophers, and doubtless better ones, to whom similar questions might be put. But readers of an autobiography by a priest who has spent years in philosophical studies and writing might reasonably expect to be treated to something more than a travelogue or a series of anecdotes.

When asked the question mentioned above, I think that Cardinal Heenan replied by employing a distinction, well known to moral theologians and spiritual counsellors, between doubt and difficulty, a distinction which had been made by J.H. Newman in his *Apologia Pro Vita Sua* (chapter 5), when he stated that "ten thousand difficulties do not make one doubt." He had certainly been conscious of difficulties, but a hundred difficulties, he claimed, do not amount to one doubt. The sort of thing that Heenan had in mind can be explained easily enough by an example or two. Consider a student of theology, who in the course of his studies is introduced to a number of difficulties or possible objections to this or that Christian doctrine. The lecturer, let us suppose, offers solutions of the relevant problems. The student, being a bright youth, finds the alleged solutions intellectually unsatisfactory or inadequate. For him, the difficulties or problems remain unsolved. But it does not necessarily follow that he therefore doubts the truth of the relevant articles of belief. For in spite of difficulties, problems or puzzles which can be brought against certain doctrines, he may still accept the doctrines on faith, as revealed by God through the mediation of the Church. Again, many people have seen in the evil and suffering which permeate human life and history a powerful objection to belief in the existence of God as conceived in traditional Christianity. But even if a Christian is quite ready to acknowledge an inability to provide any complete solution of the so-called 'problem of evil,' he or she may nonetheless cling to faith in the divine love and providential care.

It hardly needs saying that the rationalist would take a dim view of such behaviour. In the eyes of the rationalist, if a Christian finds himself or herself unable to provide an adequate reply to a powerful objection to a given doctrine, he should at any rate suspend judgment about the truth of the doctrine in question. At the same time the rationalist would doubtless willingly admit that it is a characteristic of the genuine religious believer to fight against what he or she sees as temptations to doubt, in spite of his or her awareness of what may appear as grounds for doubt, or even of disbelief. In other words, the claim that Cardinal Heenan was referring to a distinction which is not empty or purely verbal but has been and presumably still is exemplified in actual life, can be consistently allowed even by someone who looks on the behaviour of the staunch believer as manifesting a notable lack of respect for reason and its justified demands.

Though the distinction under discussion is a real one, in the sense that it does not lack exemplification in actual life, it is arguable that it implies a concept of doubt which is narrower, more restricted than that which the term 'doubt' can bear in ordinary linguistic usage. What I have in mind is this. The distinction, as understood by Cardinal Heenan, was employed by confessors and spiritual counsellors to allay the anxieties or scruples of believers who were troubled by the thought that their

puzzling over problems relating to the meaningfulness or
truth of articles of faith was equivalent to entertaining
doubt about the truth of God's word or to calling in question revealed truth. Such persons were assured that considered in themselves, neither becoming aware of difficulties or objections relating to the meaningfulness or truth-
claims of Christian beliefs nor turning over such objections in one's mind constituted something sinful. As
Heenan put it, a hundred difficulties do not amount to
one doubt. It is implied, of course, that doubt is sinful.
But the word 'doubt' is often used in ordinary language in
a sense which would make it quite unreasonable to describe doubt as sinful. For example, if a person says,
'doubts came into my mind,' one would clearly not be justified in jumping to the conclusion that he or she had
been guilty of sin, an offence against God. In other
words, in what Cardinal Heenan said the term 'doubt'
was understood in a somewhat narrower or more restricted sense than it often is in ordinary language.
Heenan would doubtless have explained, if talked to on
the subject, that doubt, considered simply as such, without any regard to context, could not reasonably be described as an offence against God. But if, for example, a
Catholic, committed to believing that a given doctrine
was revealed by a God who can neither deceive nor be de-
ceived, were seriously to call the truth of the doctrine in
question, and still more if he or she deliberately rejected
the doctrine, his or her action could be described as sinful, as an offence against God, provided at any rate that
certain conditions were fulfilled, a matter which might be
known only by God. Heenan was perfectly well aware, of
course, that even the doubter may be unable to determine
with confidence that his or her activity of doubting was
or was not sinful, or, if it was, in what degree. The Cardinal was actually making an autobiographical remark in
reply to a question about his own personal experience.
He had often had 'difficulties,' problems, puzzles; but he
had not seriously called in question the truth of doctrines
which he had been brought up to regard as expressing divine revelation.

When one is thinking about doubt in the religious sphere, it is natural to understand it as referring primarily to specific religious beliefs. There are doubtless plenty of people who would certainly describe themselves as Christians but who either doubt or reject the doctrine of hell. Catholic theologians may have condemned the policy of picking and choosing, maintaining that to deny one article of faith is to deny them all. But many Christians do not think in this way. For example, while once Protestants were brought up to reject the idea of purgatory but believe in the doctrine of hell, it is now common enough to accept some version of the idea of purgatory but reject or call in question the doctrine of hell. Again, there are those, I assume, who do not believe in the Virgin Birth of Christ, but who claim to believe in the Resurrection.

In the case of accepting or rejecting a specific religious belief or doctrine a great deal depends on how the doctrine in question is understood. Consider the doctrine of hell. I remember that I once gave a lecture on hell in the Senate House of the University of London in place of the then professor of the philosophy of religion, who was absent at the time. In the course of the lecture I emphasized the difficulty in reconciling this doctrine (if understood as involving the claim that the divine Judge will sentence a greater or lesser number of human beings to never-ending torments by way of punishment for sin) with belief in a God of love, unless one is prepared to find the concept of divine love being reduced to vacuity, by being progressively converted into a term devoid of any definite meaning. After the lecture an engaging Nonconformist student came up to me and spoke more or less as follows. "From what you said in your lecture, you seem to accept the idea of heaven, while rejecting or at any rate feeling doubt about the doctrine of hell. But surely in the Scriptures the two ideas go together, and you cannot accept the one without the other." My reply was, if I remember correctly, "You are quite right of course. As the Bishop of Woolwich (i.e., Dr. John A.T. Robinson) has reminded us, we must preserve both sides of the myth, as expressing the vital importance in life of the Either/Or, the basic choice for or against God." I suspect that the good young man was a biblical fundamentalist, and I dare say that he found this answer less than edifying. What I was suggesting was that while the doctrine of hell is unacceptable if understood in certain ways, it is not necessary to understand it in such a form. Possession of freedom implies that the human being can accept or reject God. And while I am powerfully attracted by the idea of the return of the Many to the One, of the eventual union of all human beings with God (without their obliteration), I do not see how one can exclude the possibility of a human being persisting in his or her choice against God and so remaining in a state of alienation from God. Given this possibility, hell would be more something chosen by the human being in question, than simply imposed by a ruthless judge. But this line of thought is open to a number of weighty objections, and I incline to what seems to have been Dr. Robinson's interpretation, namely of the pictorial ideas of heaven and hell as constituting together "a way of encouraging human beings to make the fundamental and all-important option for God."

Bertrand Russell says somewhere that if a cleric feels that he is losing or has lost his faith, he redefines it. And it may seem that to some extent I resemble Russell's cleric. But in the case of the doctrine of hell the young man whom I mentioned made a sound point when he argued that the ideas of heaven and hell are complementary, and that if the one idea expresses revelation, so does the other. The orthodox Christian can be expected to accept both; and I do accept them. But it seems to me that in the Scriptures the ideas are expressed in ways designed to influence life and conduct, and that to interpret them in that light is clearly justifiable. To this line of thought I shall return shortly in a broader or more general context. Meanwhile I wish to make the following remarks.

When I look back on my life up to date, it seems to me that incipient doubts about the truth of this or that Christian belief as distinct from others has not played any very conspicuous role. I am more aware of experiencing general impressions of the unreality of the Christian vision or interpretation of reality in general. Sometimes, indeed, the Christian faith has seemed, and from time to time, does seem, pretty preposterous. It can, of course, be argued that if by 'Christian faith' I understand the totality of Christian beliefs, any incipient doubts must necessarily refer to particular doctrines. There is, however, a difference between having some particular doctrines at the forefront of one's mind and having a general impression of the Christian vision reality as not representing reality as it is actually known by us. Doubt about the truth of specific beliefs *a* and *b* does not necessarily imply doubts in regard to the truth of beliefs *c* and *d*. But in the experience of which I am thinking it is a general picture, structure or map, which appears as an unrealistic representation of the world in which we live. It is, I suppose, more appropriate to refer to the impression as a temptation to doubt or as providing a point of departure for doubt than as being itself a doubt; but one might perhaps describe the mental impression as incipient doubt.

It is not my intention to suggest that this sort of impression is a rare occurrence, still less that it is confined to myself. I assume that it is common enough, though varying, of course, in intensity and duration. In my own case, though I would not describe the impression as a violently tormenting experience, its incidence seems to me to belong more to later than to earlier years; and I suppose that it is or may well be, in large part at any rate, a result of prolonged study of a wide spectrum of philosophical thought. This could hardly fail to exercise some influence on one's mind in one or more ways. By saying this I do not intend to express regret at having studied, for example, logical positivism. For an historian of philosophy who is also a Christian believer to confine his or her studies to the philosophies or philosophical traditions which supported or at any rate were compatible with the historian's religious beliefs would be, in my opinion, absurd. But this does not alter the fact that serious study, embodying a genuine effort to understand, can be ex-

214 / *Memoirs of a Philosopher*

pected to have some effect on the historian's mind. It need not necessarily weaken the historian's personal faith. It may simply increase his understanding of positions other than his own. In my case, however, I think that it has certainly contributed to the occurrence from time to time of the sort of general impression to which I have referred above.

Not long after the death of A.J. Ayer I was told by an American friend of Ayer that the philosopher had liked to relate 'in private' that he had succeeded in bringing me by argument to abandon Christian belief. This puzzled me. For one thing, though I certainly discussed with Ayer such topics as the principle of verifiability as a criterion of meaning, I do not recollect ever having discussed with him Christianity specifically. For another thing, I was unable to think of any ground which I had given him for claiming that he had induced me to abandon Christian belief. In the end I came to the conclusion that his statement, as reported to me, was more an expression of what he would like to have happened than of what actually happened. I suspected that Ayer's claim in regard to myself had been a rather light-hearted contribution to an after-dinner conversation. In a sense, of course, Ayer may have regarded his statement as a compliment to me, implying, that is to say, that I had the open-mindedness and honesty to recognize 'the light' and part company with a load of nonsense. In actual fact, however, I remained a Christian believer, whatever my friend Freddie Ayer might like to think. My faith has certainly undergone strains at times, and I am inclined to think that with advancing years the strains have grown more noticeable rather than less; but it has not, I hope, evaporated.

In his work *The Life of E.F. Benson* the author, Brian Masters, says of Lucia, a character in one of Benson's novels (*Queen Lucia*) that "she believes in God in much the same way as she believes in Australia." (p. 237) While, however, there may well have been people, whose professed belief in God has resembled that attributed to Lucia in Benson's novel, the kind of belief in question hardly measures up to the ideal of Christian faith in God. For this involves or expresses self-commitment to God as a loving Father. It is considerably more than reasoned assent to the statement that the idea of God is exemplified. Let us assume that there are good reasons for believing that the concept of a water-buffalo is exemplified and that there are no sufficient reasons for believing otherwise. The fact remains that one can perfectly well believe in the existence of water-buffaloes without one's life being notably affected thereby and without anyone expecting that one's life should be affected by the belief alone. Obviously, in certain countries the existence of water-buffaloes can make an important practical difference to people's lives. At the same time an Englishman, say, or a Frenchman can perfectly well believe that the concept of a water-buffalo is exemplified without his being expected to maintain a personal relationship with any water-buffalo. Christian faith in God, however, to be itself, to be, that is to say, *Christian* faith, is rightly expected to issue in self-commitment to God and ideally at any rate, in the leading of a certain kind of life. It is natural, therefore, for the committed Christian to see the struggle to preserve faith, in the face of all temptations to abandon it, as demanded by personal loyalty to God, manifested in and through Jesus of Nazareth.

The rationalist need not, of course, deny that the committed Christian conceives faith in God as something more than a bare intellectual assent to the claim that the idea of God is exemplified. But he would presumably maintain that if someone believes in God and if subsequently reasons for doubting or denying the truth of this belief present themselves to the person's mind, genuine respect for reason demands that he or she should examine the relevant reasons in an objective manner, dispassionately weighing pros and cons, instead of treating the reasons as 'temptations' and trying to dismiss them, on the ground that to entertain them deliberately would be sinful. The Russian philosopher Leon Shestov (Lev Isaakovich Schwarzman) maintained that any attempt to justify religion before the tribunal of reason leads inevitably to the complete victory of reason over religion. We can well imagine the hard-boiled rationalist commenting "precisely!" and expressing strong disapprobation of Shestov's call for the leap of faith, for an uncompromising adherence to Jerusalem rather than Athens, in the sphere of religion, that is to say.

In the foregoing remarks I have obviously understood rationalism and Christian faith as sharply opposed positions. The former I have understood as demanding that before any religious belief is accepted it should be brought before the tribunal of reason and submitted to a stringent examination, while the latter, as mention of Shestov makes clear, has been understood as demanding a leap of faith. In other words, though the two positions, as so presented, are, indeed, sharply opposed, they nonetheless have this feature in common, that compromise, adoption of a middle position, is rejected. That is to say, as far as religion is concerned, people are summoned to choose between reason and faith, Athens and Jerusalem.

When I refer to a 'middle position' in this context I am mainly thinking of a religiously oriented metaphysics, conceived as a construction of reason but at the same time as looking forward to Christian faith. That is to say, the metaphysics would not only leave room for faith by abstaining from claiming the ability to take over and absorb in itself the whole range of religious truth, thereby converting faith into philosophy; it would also embody dynamic orientation of the human spirit, a movement towards a transcendent reality. While I may once have thought in terms of a determinate metaphysical system, serving, so to speak, as a lower storey in a building culminating in the grasp by faith of revealed truth, in the course of time I have become increasingly influenced by the idea of philosophy's movement of self-criticism and self-limitation, as puncturing determinate systems and thus facilitating, though not necessitating, a reaching out towards an ultimate reality transcending all that is visible or that can be conceptually mastered, though it can be thought in terms of analogies. I am well aware that my efforts to express this line of thought are open to objection and criticism. Given, however, my growing mistrust of dogmatic philosophical systems, this does not bother me much. If the line of thought in question discourages dogmatic assertion of the final truth of some determinate metaphysical system, it also discourages the confining and, in my opinion, impoverishing activity not of reason as such but of dogmatic rationalism. The emphasis which I have come to lay in my own mind on the self-critical function of philosophical thought may make it easier to accommodate the idea of religious faith as involving an element of venture and self-commitment to the living God.

At this point I wish to reflect on my own life of faith from a rather different angle. Not so very long ago I gave a short talk entitled 'The Faith of a Philosopher.' I began by remarking that the title was potentially misleading. For it might be taken to imply that a philosopher who claims to be a Christian believer has or can be expected to have some special kind of faith, one that is different from that of believers who are not philosophers. When, however, Catholics recite the Creed at Mass, they nowadays begin with the words "We believe in . . . ," a phrase which clearly implies that, ideally at any rate, all the members of the Church share a common faith. At the same time, as I proceeded to remark, as people obviously differ in a variety of ways, in their intellectual capacities and ideas, in their emotive reactions, in their experience of life, it is only to be expected that some differences should be discernible between their several ways of understanding, appropriating and reacting to shared beliefs, even though the truths of faith can be stated in an abstract manner, as in catechisms and theological textbooks, the common uniting faith is received, understood and held in and by persons who are not simply replicas of one another.

This clearly applies to philosophers as well as to non-philosophers. Philosophers are human beings, and as human beings differ, so do philosophers. Instead, therefore, of laying down the law about philosophers in general, I intend to put forward a largely personal point of

view. Needless to say, while some readers may sympathize with what I say about faith, other readers may disagree with it, dislike it, or dismiss it as an expression of
senility.

It hardly needs saying that if articles of faith are to
be proposed for belief, they have to be expressed in language. And even if the philosopher is not qualified to set
himself up as an authority on what a Christian should
believe, we can hardly forbid him to raise questions relating, for example, to truth-claims and to problems of
meaning. It is not necessarily a case of purely hostile polemics, with no real attempt at establishing mutual understanding. If discussion expresses a genuine search for
truth on both sides, there can be a fruitful dialogue.
Though, however, it is natural to think of dialogue as oc-
curring between two or more persons, it may also take
place within the consciousness of one and the same person. To be sure, this kind of interior dialogue is probably
set going and fed through the influence of various external factors (for instance, by what other people have written or said), but the dialogue can nonetheless develop
within the mind of a single person. We might speak of a
dialogue between critical or questioning reason on the one
hand and Christian faith on the other. In spite of what
Shestov claimed, the result of such a dialogue need not be
the surrender of one's faith. It could be, for example, a
somewhat altered understanding of the nature of Christian faith.

When reflecting in advanced years on certain Catholic doctrines, such as the real presence of the risen Christ
in the Blessed Sacrament, I have sometimes wondered to
what extent, if any, I, Frederick Copleston, could honestly
claim to understand them. The further question then
arose in my mind, can one justifiably claim to believe in
the truth of an assertion, if one seriously wonders
whether one understands what the assertion means?
This sort of question can, of course, be treated as a general logical problem, without any specific reference to religious doctrines. But for present purposes the relevant

context is that of the relation between critical reason and Christian faith.

A well instructed Catholic might at once remind me that doctrines such as those of the Trinity and real presence are said to be 'mysteries,' transcending the human mind's power of comprehension, and that in this case it is no matter for surprise if one's understanding of them is defective. While, however, this is quite true, as far as it goes, I surely cannot reasonably claim to believe in the truth of an assertion, unless I am confident that I understand *something*, that I can attach *some* meaning to it, even if it is simply a matter of being able to distinguish between the relevant assertion and its contradictory, between p and *non-p*. To assert, for example, that God is three Persons in one Nature, and to claim that Christ is really present in the Eucharist is to exclude his not being present. There does not seem to be any difficulty in grasping the meaning of such claims.

Well, I can certainly grasp the logical point that a meaningful assertion excludes its contradictory. But I may nonetheless wonder whether I can honestly claim to have sufficient understanding of a given putative assertion in order to be able to claim justifiably that I believe in the truth of the assertion. That is to say, I may feel doubtful whether, if someone asks me, with reference to my claim to believe a given doctrine, "But what is it that you believe is true?" I am in a position to give a clear answer. Let us suppose that someone says to me "You say that you believe that p is true, but can you tell me clearly, without simply repeating the formulation of p, what it is that you believe to be true?" And let us suppose that I feel compelled to answer, "No, I cannot possibly give you a clear account. For, you see, p expresses a mystery, transcending my power of understanding." It would not be altogether surprising, if my questioner were to draw the conclusion that I do not really know what it is that I claim to believe. The question then arises, whether I can justifiably claim to believe in the truth of an assertion, when I have to admit and do admit, that the meaning of the assertion is not clear to me.

Reflection on this familiar line of thought prompted me to try another approach to what seemed to be a somewhat embarrassing situation. If we assume that God revealed a number of truths principally in order to increase our knowledge by imparting information which we could not otherwise acquire, we might understandably feel aggrieved that he did not make the content of the information a bit clearer, instead of leaving it in the darkness of obscurity or shrouded in mystery. But did not Christ claim to have come as the Light of the world, to enable human beings to attain eternal life by living a certain kind of life, the life of Christian love, as portrayed in the Gospels? In other words, may we not see divine revelation as geared, so to speak, not so much to the imparting of information for its own sake as to the leading of a certain kind of life?

The point which I am trying to make is that if a given doctrine is capable of stimulating one sort of conduct rather than another, it can hardly be devoid of meaning. If, for example, the doctrine of the real presence of Christ in the Eucharist is capable of encouraging a life of active love, rather than hostility and enmity, between members of the Church, it must clearly possess sufficient meaning to produce or promote this effect. If, nonetheless, the sacramental presence of Christ remains mysterious, with hidden depths, this may help to focus our attention on what Christ came to *do* in us and through us. After all, God did not reveal this or that truth simply to impart some more or less interesting information. Revelation was granted for salvation, to bring human beings to union with God; and Christ is recorded as saying that he came that human beings might have life—and have it more abundantly. It seems to me therefore that in our interpretation of Christianity we would do well to lay stress on life, on leading the kind of life preached by Christ, as recorded in the Gospels. It is not a question of discarding or throwing overboard the idea of divine revelation of truth. It is a question of where we are to place the emphasis. And with the advance of years I have become increasingly convinced that in interpreting the Christian faith we should place the emphasis where, as it seems to me, Jesus placed it, namely on the leading of a life of Christian love. Problems of meaning can certainly be raised in regard to Christian doctrines, problems which provide ample matter for discussion between theologians on the one hand and questioning philosophers on the other; but it seems clear to me that if Christian doctrine is capable of promoting or encouraging the leading of one kind of life rather than another, it must be meaningful, with a meaning which can be grasped not only by theologians but also by ordinary people, the sort of simple people to whom Christ preached.

My adoption of the foregoing line of thought may give some readers (if there are any readers) the impression that I have embraced, or am well on the way to embracing, the position taken by the Cambridge philosopher R.B. Braithwaite in his well known lecture entitled 'An Empiricist's View of the Nature of Religious Belief.' This impression, however, would be mistaken. Braithwaite, having accepted logical positivism as a philosophy in tune with modern science, became powerfully attracted to Christianity and received Christian baptism. As he persisted in adherence to logical positivism or empiricism, he tried to combine or harmonize the two, and this meant that in his interpretation of Christianity he had to follow a reductionist programme. The essence of Christianity was seen as personal commitment to follow an 'agapeistic' way of life, a life of Christian love, that is to say, while Christian statements about God, to fit in with the logical positivist theory of meaning, were regarded as being neither true nor false. As for myself, while I certainly sympathize with the emphasis which he laid on commitment to trying to lead a life of Christian love, I am not a logical positivist and am not prepared to describe Christian statements about God as being neither true nor false. In other words, I do not accept the logical positivist theory of meaning, and I have written and argued against it. Nor am I a reductionist, interpreting statements about God as being 'really' moral imperatives. To be sure, I am aware that my own position is open to criticism, and I am far from confident that I can cope successfully with all possible objections; but this does not alter the fact that I do not accept the theory of meaning, adherence to which compelled Braithwaite to regard talk about God as a 'story' which one tells oneself to support Christian moral commitment but which does not refer to an existing transcendent reality.

It is doubtless true that my reflection on logical positivism and the like has had an influence on my mind. But I do not think that in the sphere of religious belief this influence has had the effect of leading me either to abandon faith in God or to translate talk about God into talk about something else, while retaining use of the word 'God.' On the contrary, I think that my dialogue with positivism in various forms has stimulated me to defend attempts to develop a general world-view in which the idea of a movement of the human spirit towards increasing union with, or return to, a transcendent One through an increasing union of active love with one's fellows is central and of great importance. I understand that this line of thought lies open to criticism and attack from various angles. But so, of course, do the claims and dogmas of positivist, anti-metaphysical philosophy. In any case my dialogue with anti-religious philosophy has not led me either to discard or to belittle Christian faith in God. On the contrary, it seems to me to have contributed, in the long run, to a clearer appreciation of the spirit of the Christian religion and of the orientation of divine self-revelation to promoting a way of life, a life of active love, of overcoming alienation of the human person from other persons and from God, the two being aspects of one movement.

It by no means follows, of course, that what I am inclined to think of as an understanding of where the emphasis should be placed in one's view of the Christian life and its demands is necessarily accompanied by an increase in Christian practice. It seems to me to be more a matter of becoming increasingly aware of where one's deplorable failure, one's falling short of Christian standards is principally to be located. Up to a point this is, I sup-

pose, an advance. At the same time increasing awareness of one's failure, past and present, to practice Christian love is not the same thing as becoming increasingly
loving towards all. As for myself, it seems to me that I
become more unloving, more self-centred, rather than
less. But it may be not so much a case of one's becoming
worse than one used to be as of the circumstances of old
age, such as the unavoidable curtailing of one's outwards-
directed activities, causing one to become more conscious
of ingrained character-defects. To be sure, this line of
thought may seem discouraging or pessimistic, in the
sense that it suggests that one is unable to do much, if
anything, to improve matters. That is to say, it may appear that while one may become more clear-sighted in regard to one's basic shortcomings, it may also be the case
that one becomes less rather than more capable of bringing about a radical change in oneself. At the same time
an increasing sense of one's inability to bring about a
radical conversion in oneself may have the salutary effect
of leading one to abandon oneself into the hands of God.
For the believer, of course, one is there in any case, but
perhaps the onset of old age should make an act of complete self-abandonment to God somewhat easier. I hope
at any rate that this is the case.

Let me bring these Memoirs to a close. It should be
clear from what I have written that I welcome what I see
as a change of emphasis in the Church from preoccupation with doctrinal orthodoxy to laying stress on the call
to live the life of love which Christ is represented in the
Gospels as demanding of his disciples. At the same time
there is a recognizably Christian vision of reality, which
is, or should be, a uniting factor among members of the
Christian community. To emphasize the life of love is not
the same thing as claiming that the idea of a common
faith should be thrown out of the window. As for the life
of love, when I spoke about this as a central ideal of
Christianity, I was not thinking exclusively of relations
between individual members of a family or between individuals as such, still less of heated emotive attitudes.
Realization of a truly Christian world, embodying the

224 / Memoirs of a Philosopher

to overcome social injustice and the transcending of war
as a means of settling disputes or differences between nations. To be sure, it is by no means always clear what is
the best way of tackling a given social injustice, and
there may be different opinions whether a given situation
should or should not be regarded as a concrete example of
social injustice. At the same time the Christian ideal of
love is that of an active love, contributing not only to establishment of better relations between individuals as
such but also to the realization of a harmoniously united
world-society.

"It is all very well," someone might say, "to talk
about the need for looking to the future and contributing
to the building-up of a better world, a more just and
harmoniously united society; but have you not spent
much of your adult life looking backwards and recon-
structing the past, rather than in endeavouring to shape
the future for the benefit of mankind?" A cynic might
perhaps comment that preoccupation with the past has at
any rate kept me from making a persistent nuisance of
myself to other people by urging them to do what they
have no inclination to do and no intention of doing. But
it is quite true, of course, that I have spent a great deal
of time in studying the past and in writing and talking
about it. And I must admit that at times I have felt inclined to think that I have wasted much of my life. But
it would be foolish to dwell on such thoughts. Apart from
the fact that in occupying myself with the historical development of philosophical thought I have done, by and
large, what my Superiors wished me to do, it is rash to
assume that study of the past is necessarily irrelevant to
life and action in the present. After all, historical study
is study of some aspect of the one developing world in
which we live and act. However this may be, the only really important evaluation of one's life and work is God's
evaluation. And in the closing years of one's life it is just
as well to bear this in mind.

Index